LUNCHEON AND SUPPER DISHES

LUNCHEON AND SUPPER DISHES

Selected by

EULALIA BLAIR

Jule Wilkinson, Editor

Published by
INSTITUTIONS/VOLUME FEEDING MAGAZINE

Distributed by
Cahners Books, 89 Franklin St., Boston, Mass. 02110

Library of Congress Catalog Card No. 72-92379
ISBN 0-8436-0559-6

Printed in the United States of America

TABLE OF CONTENTS

INTRODUCTION   1

SOUPS   2

CHEESE DISHES   16

VEGETABLE ENTREES   26

EGG DISHES   40

PASTA AND RICE   54

SANDWICHES   80

SALADS   104

POULTRY   126

FISH AND SEAFOOD   142

MEAT   170

ACKNOWLEDGEMENTS

The recipes on the following pages reflect the creative thinking of many minds. And there are many people to thank for these recipes, for their down-to-earth practical qualities and for the imaginative features that set them apart.

I should like to express my most sincere "Thank you" to the skillful technicians who have worked in the various test kitchens to develop and perfect the recipes. And to my business and professional associates allied with food processors, manufacturers, public relations firms, advertising agencies, associations and institutions who, over the years, have given unstintingly of their counsel and cooperation to supply the recipe material that was such a valuable part of Volume Feeding Management Magazine. And, I should like to thank them again for furnishing the photographs that illustrate this book.

I also want to voice my appreciation to the foodservice operators across the nation who, time and time again, shared treasured recipes from their kitchens.

In addition, I want to gratefully acknowledge the capable help of Book Editor, Mrs. Jule Wilkinson in designing, editing and handling endless details concerned with publishing.

Eulalia C. Blair

INTRODUCTION

This cookbook is designed to help the women and men in the foodservice field who have the responsibility for planning menus and for providing the kitchen staff with reliable recipes to carry them out. More specifically, it is intended to offer a hand to people who—at least part of the time—find the planning of luncheon and supper dishes easier said than done.

All of the recipes come from the large and well-regarded collection that derives from the Recipe File section in former issues of Volume Feeding Management (now the combined Institutions/Volume Feeding Management Magazine).

The book is divided into ten sections under the headings of Soups, Sandwiches, Salads, Vegetables, Rice and Pasta, Eggs, Cheese, Fish and Seafood, Poultry, and Meats. Each chapter is filled with unusual and exciting entree recipes that range from the homey type to the gourmet. The recipes were chosen with luncheon or supper service in mind. At the same time the factors of variety, practicality and broad appeal came in for their share of earnest attention. Many recipes take advantage of shortcuts, are sparing of time and careful of cost.

This was not intended as a menu cookbook. Nor is it. But, as the recipe selection began to take form, the idea of proposing teammates seemed a happy thought. And so each recipe carries a brief caption which describes the item or offers ideas for menu companions. You can follow the suggestions or change them about. Hopefully, they will help initiate lively —and successful—ideas of your own.

Seafood Chowder (top)—recipe, p. 4
Cape Cod Fish Chowder (below)—recipe, p. 12

Shrimp Association of the Americas

SOUPS

A SUPER soup, reinforced with meat, seafood, vegetables or other hearty bits of food, can set the stage for a delightful luncheon or light evening menu.

A bowl of soup that's thick, satisfying and abounding in nourishment can be—and usually is—far too filling to eat with a meal. But, served as a main course with support from accessories, these robust soups can rise to full stature, become meals in themselves.

It is easy to work out attractive menus starring a soup with a salad and an interesting bread. Or, with a simple sandwich and a dish of relishes. The many kinds of crackers available today give tremendous leeway for change and variety—to say nothing of breadsticks, corn chips, hot breads and rolls.

Sandwiches, salads and relishes, likewise, hold an enormous potential for providing a pleasing accent and supplementing the meal. And, last but not least, let's not overlook the part a well-chosen dessert can play in rounding out an inviting menu that you plan around soup.

SEAFOOD CHOWDER
(Picture on page 2)

Try presenting with hot popovers. Then let lemon pie settle the question, "And what's for dessert?"

Yield: 25 portions

Ingredients

OLIVE OIL	1/2 cup
ONIONS, chopped	2/3 cup
GARLIC, minced	4 cloves
CLAM BROTH	2 quarts
TOMATOES, fresh, peeled, chopped*	2 quarts
CARROTS, finely chopped	2 cups
CELERY, chopped	1 quart
SALT	2 teaspoons
THYME, crumbled	1 tablespoon
BAY LEAVES	6 to 8
SHRIMP, shelled, deveined	3 pounds
SCALLOPS	3 pounds

Procedure

1. Heat oil in heavy kettle. Add onion and garlic; saute until tender but not brown.
2. Add clam broth, vegetables, salt, thyme and bay leaves. Simmer, uncovered, 45 minutes, stirring occasionally.
3. Add raw shrimp and scallops; simmer 10 minutes.
4. Serve in soup bowls. Garnish with chopped parsley, if desired.

*Or, canned tomatoes, drained.

IRISH SOUP DINNER

Small buttermilk biscuits go well with this soup. So does a molded pear salad and following it, a butterscotch sundae.

Yield: 3 gallons

Ingredients

BEEF SHORT RIBS, cross-cut, cut in 2-inch pieces	8 pounds
ONION SOUP MIX	2 6-ounce cans
WATER	2 gallons
CARROTS, cut in ½-inch lengths	3 pounds
POTATOES, peeled, quartered	4½ pounds
CELERY, cut in 1-inch lengths	1¼ pounds

SCALLOP STEW

Nice with bread sticks or pilot crackers, tossed green salad with crumbled cheese and warm deep-dish apple pie.

Yield: Approximately 2½ gallons

Ingredients

BUTTER OR MARGARINE	1 pound
FLOUR	8 ounces (2 cups)
SALT	3 to 4 tablespoons
PEPPER	2½ teaspoons
ONION, diced	8 ounces
CELERY SALT	1 teaspoon
CAYENNE	dash
LIQUID INSTANT NONFAT DRY MILK*	1 gallon, 2½ quarts
LIQUID NONDAIRY CREAMER*	1½ quarts
SCALLOPS, frozen, thawed, drained	5 pounds
CHIVES, chopped	as needed

Procedure

1. Melt butter; add flour and seasonings; blend.
2. Cook and stir over low heat 3 to 5 minutes, until smooth and bubbly.
3. Add liquid milk and non dairy creamer, stirring constantly. Bring to a boil; cook and stir until thickened.
4. Cut scallops in bite-size pieces. Add to milk mixture. Simmer, over low heat, about 10 minutes. Serve garnished with chives.
*Prepared according to package directions.

Procedure

1. Place meat, soup mix and water in steam-jacketed kettle. Cover; cook 1½ hours.
2. Add vegetables; cook, covered, 30 minutes, or until meat and vegetables are tender. Skim off excess fat.

ORIENTAL CHICKEN SOUP DINNER

Team with a salad of crisp greens and sliced avocado. Offer chilled pineapple chunks and sugar cookies for dessert.

Yield: 3 gallons

Ingredients

CHICKEN NOODLE SOUP MIX	2 10-ounce cans
WATER, boiling	1¾ gallons
CHINESE VEGETABLES, mixed (canned)	3 quarts
CHICKEN, cooked, cut in pieces	4½ pounds (2¼ quarts)
SCALLIONS, sliced	2 cups

Procedure

1. Stir soup mix into boiling water. Cook 10 minutes.
2. Add undrained Chinese vegetables and chicken; cook 5 minutes.
3. Stir in scallions; serve.

CONTINENTAL CREAM SOUP

As menu mates for this distinctive cream soup, try suggesting an orange waldorf salad, toasted English muffins and coconut custard pie.

Yield: 40 8-ounce portions

Ingredients

FLOUR	6 ounces (1½ cups)
SALT	2 tablespoons
CHERVIL	2 teaspoons
PEPPER	1 teaspoon
BUTTER OR MARGARINE, melted	1½ pounds
MILK, hot	1¼ gallons
LETTUCE, finely chopped	1 quart
HAM, cooked, finely chopped	12 ounces
EGGS, well beaten	8
CREAM, heavy	1 quart
PEAS, drained	1 No. 10 can

Procedure

1. Blend flour, seasonings and melted butter. Gradually add part of the milk; stir until smooth.
2. Add remaining milk, lettuce and ham. Cook over low heat, stirring frequently, about 20 minutes or until slightly thickened.
3. Blend eggs and cream; stir into hot soup. Add drained peas. Heat, stirring frequently, for several more minutes but do not boil. Serve hot.

HAM CHOWDER

This hearty, flavorful soup suggests corn sticks, a deviled egg salad and a fruit compote to complete the meal.

Yield: 50 1-cup portions

Ingredients

ONION, chopped	1 pound, 2 ounces
BUTTER OR MARGARINE	6 ounces
POTATOES, diced	6 pounds
HAM, cooked, coarsely chopped	2 pounds
SALT	4½ tablespoons
WORCESTERSHIRE SAUCE	2 tablespoons
THYME	1½ teaspoons
PAPRIKA	½ teaspoon
CELERY SALT	1½ teaspoons
WATER, boiling	3½ quarts
MILK, hot	1¼ gallons
FLOUR, all-purpose	¾ cup
WATER, cold	1 cup
PEAS, cooked	1 pound (2½ cups)
PARSLEY, chopped	¾ cup

Procedure

1. Saute onion in butter until lightly browned.
2. Combine onion, potatoes, ham, seasonings and boiling water. Cook 15 minutes or until vegetables are done.
3. Add hot milk.
4. Blend flour and cold water to make a thin, smooth paste. Stir into hot mixture; continue cooking gently until slightly thickened.
5. Add peas; heat thoroughly.
6. Serve garnished with parsley.

SOUP GARNISHES

Crumbled bacon
Snipped chipped beef
Shrimp, split lengthwise
Thin slices of King crab legs
Thin, narrow strips of salami
Sliced frankfurters
Tiny meat balls
Shredded cheese
Croutons—plain, herbed or
   with cheese

Tiny unfilled cream puffs
Oysterettes or goldfish crackers
Cooked shell macaroni
Rosettes of Duchess potato
Toasted sliced almonds
French fried onion rings
Chinese noodles
Sliced mushrooms
Cooked green peas
Shredded raw carrot

FISH-CORN CHOWDER

This robust chowder combines easily with a crisp cabbage slaw or the crunch of chilled fresh vegetable relishes.

Yield: 24–1½ cup portions

Ingredients

WATER	1¾ quarts
SALT	2½ tablespoons
BAY LEAVES	3
HADDOCK OR COD	4½ pounds
POTATOES	2¼ pounds
BACON	1 pound, 2 ounces
ONION, thinly sliced	4½ cups, (22½ ounces)
FLOUR	1½ cups (6 ounces)
PEPPER, black, ground	¾ teaspoon
NUTMEG, ground	½ teaspoon
CORN, whole kernel	2¼ pounds
CREAM, light, scalded	1 quart
MILK, scalded	1½ quarts
PARSLEY, snipped	1½ cups
SALTINE CRACKERS and soup and oyster crackers	as needed

Procedure

1. Add water, salt and bay leaves to fish. Bring to a boil. Reduce heat; simmer 8 to 10 minutes or until done. Remove fish. Reserve stock.

2. Cut potatoes into small cubes; cook in salted water until almost tender; drain.

3. Fry bacon until crisp; remove; crumble. Saute onion in bacon fat until tender. Blend in flour. Add fish stock, pepper and nutmeg, stirring until smooth. Cook and stir until thickened.

4. Add fish, bacon, potatoes and corn. Heat thoroughly.

5. Stir in hot cream and milk. Sprinkle with parsley.

6. Serve with saltine crackers and soup and oyster crackers.

Fish-Corn Chowder

Nabisco, Inc.

CORN CHOWDER

Toasted slices of rye bread provide a nice complement for this tasty chowder. For a heartier offering, team the soup with a sandwich made with Swiss cheese, corned beef and cress.

Yield: 50 1-cup portions

Ingredients

POTATOES, diced	2¼ quarts
ONIONS, chopped	2 cups
WATER	1 gallon
MILK, whole	2 gallons
BACON OR SALT PORK, diced	1 pound
FLOUR, all purpose	2 cups
SALT	¼ cup
CORN, whole-kernel, cooked	1½ quarts

Procedure

1. Cook potatoes and onion in water until tender.
2. Add milk.
3. Cook bacon or salt pork until crisp. Blend in flour and salt.
4. Stir flour mixture into milk mixture. Cook until thickened slightly, stirring occasionally.
5. Add corn; heat thoroughly.

OLD-FASHIONED BEAN SOUP

Serve with king-size crackers and a smokey cheese spread as the mainstay of a meal. Add a marinated sliced tomato salad, and pumpkin pie as the dessert.

Yield: 50 10-ounce portions

Ingredients

GREAT NORTHERN BEANS	5 pounds
WATER	4 gallons
HAM BONES (meaty)	2
ONIONS, finely chopped	3 cups
BAY LEAVES	4
GARLIC, minced	6 cloves
MASHED POTATOES	1 quart
CELERY, thinly sliced	1 quart
CARROTS, diced	1 quart
SALT	as needed
PEPPER	as needed

NEW ORLEANS GUMBO

Feature with olives, celery and carrot sticks and applesauce a la mode.
Include hot Southern corn sticks for a heartier meal.

Yield: 1¾ gallons (28 8-ounce portions)

Ingredients

BAY LEAVES	8 to 10
OKRA, frozen or fresh, cut in ¼ inch to ½ inch slices	2½ pounds
ONIONS, chopped	2 cups
GREEN PEPPER, chopped	1 cup
THYME LEAF, crushed	2 tablespoons
LIQUID HOT PEPPER SEASONING	¼ teaspoon
WATER	3 quarts
TOMATO SOUP, condensed	2 51-ounce cans
SHRIMP, cooked, diced	2 pounds
RICE, cooked	2 quarts

Procedure

1. Break bay leaves into pieces; tie in a cheese cloth bag.
2. Add bay leaves, okra, onions, green pepper, thyme and pepper seasoning to water. Cook until okra is tender, 15 to 20 minutes.
3. Stir in soup and shrimp. Simmer a few minutes to blend flavors. Remove bay leaves; thin to desired consistency.
4. Garnish portions with a No. 20 scoop of rice.

Procedure

1. Wash beans. Soak overnight in measured amount of water.
2. Add ham bones, onions, bay leaves and garlic. Bring to boiling Reduce heat; cover tightly; simmer about 2 hours or until beans are al most tender.
3. Stir in mashed potatoes; add celery and carrots. Season with salt and pepper. Cover; simmer 1 hour longer.
4. Remove ham bones; cut off meat. Dice meat; add to soup.
5. Heat to just below boiling, stirring carefully. Garnish portions with chopped parsley, chopped chives, grated Parmesan or cheddar cheese.

CAPE COD FISH CHOWDER
(Picture on page 2)

*Accompany with stuffed celery, cherry tomatoes and a bouquet of cress
and suggest blueberry cobbler to complete the menu.*

Yield: 25 portions

Ingredients

SALT PORK, diced	½ pound
ONIONS, thinly sliced	1¾ pounds
POTATOES, diced	4½ pounds
CELERY, chopped	1 quart
WATER, boiling	3 quarts
SALT	1 tablespoon
BLACK PEPPER, freshly ground	½ teaspoon
FISH STEAKS OR FILLETS*	8 pounds
MILK	1 gallon
BUTTER	4 ounces
PARSLEY, chopped	as needed

Procedure

1. Saute diced pork in a large kettle until crisp. Remove crisp pieces; reserve for garnish.
2. Add onions to pork fat; cook over low heat until tender but not browned.
3. Add potatoes, celery, boiling water, salt and pepper.
4. Cut fish into medium-size pieces, removing any bones and skin. Place on vegetable mixture.
5. Cover; simmer 30 minutes.
6. Add milk and butter; simmer 5 minutes.
7. Serve in soup bowls. Garnish with reserved bits of pork and chopped parsley. Serve with pilot crackers or crisp crusty bread.

*Halibut, cod or haddock.

MORE SOUP GARNISHES

Chopped parsley or chives
Diced pimiento
Thin slices of tomato
Shredded raw spinach leaves
Sliced ripe or stuffed olives
Thin shreds of green pepper
Paprika
Whipped cream or sour cream

MULLIGATAWNY SOUP

Accent International

Feature this flavorful soup with a stuffed pear salad with chutney dressing and complete the meal with a baked raisin or date rice custard pudding.

Yield: Approximately 1½ gallons

Ingredients

FAT	1 cup (½ pound)
FLOUR	2 cups (½ pound)
CURRY POWDER	2 tablespoons
STOCK, chicken or veal	1 gallon
ONIONS, finely diced	1 to 1½ cups (½ pound)
CELERY, finely diced	1 cup (4 ounces)
CARROTS, finely diced	1 cup, scant (4 ounces)
APPLES, tart; peeled and diced	2¼ cups (½ pound)
COCONUT, long shred	1 cup (4 ounces)
MACE, ground	½ teaspoon
SALT	4½ tablespoons
MONOSODIUM GLUTAMATE	1 tablespoon
MILK, hot	1½ quarts

Procedure

1. Make a roux with fat and flour; add curry powder. Add hot stock; stir constantly until sauce is thickened and smooth.

2. Add vegetables to sauce; simmer 40 minutes or until vegetables are very tender.

3. Add apples, coconut, mace and seasonings; simmer 20 minutes longer.

4. Add hot milk. Turn off steam or heat. Blend well. Taste and correct seasoning.

ITALIANO TOMATO SOUP

Excellent partner for a leafy salad, cheese and crusty bread.

Yield: 7½ quarts

Ingredients

ZUCCHINI, 1/8-inch slices, cut in half	2 pounds
SALT	2 tablespoons
OREGANO, leaf, crushed	1 tablespoon
GARLIC, granulated	½ teaspoon
WATER, boiling	3 quarts
TOMATO SOUP, condensed	2 51-ounce cans
DITALINI PASTA*, cooked	1½ quarts
	(12 ounces uncooked)
PEPPERONI, thinly sliced	8 ounces

Procedure

1. Add zucchini, salt, oregano and garlic to the boiling water. Cover; cook only until zucchini is crisp-tender.

2. Gently stir in soup. Add cooked pasta and pepperoni. Heat to a boil; simmer a few minutes to blend flavors.

*Ditalini, a short tubular macaroni. If desired, use other small novelty macaroni.

POTATO CHOWDER

To accompany this hearty soup, offer toasted cheese bread, crisp radishes and celery hearts.

Yield: 65 6-ounce portions

Ingredients

BACON, sliced	2 1/2 pounds
INSTANT POTATO SLICES	2 1/4 pounds
ONIONS, chopped	1 pound
SALT	1/3 to 1/2 cup
PEPPER, white, ground	1 tablespoon
WATER	2 gallons
BACON FAT	1-1/3 cups
FLOUR, all-purpose	1-1/3 cups
MILK, whole, hot	2-1/4 gallons
PARSLEY, chopped	3/4 cup

CHICKEN VEGETABLE CHOWDER
Try combining with a fruit salad, Melba toast and a choice of desserts.

Yield: 2 gallons

Ingredients

CHICKEN SOUP BASE	1 cup (8 ounces)
WATER	2 quarts
CELERY, chopped	1½ cups
ONIONS, chopped	1½ cups
CARROTS, diced	1½ cups
POTATOES, diced	1½ cups
SHORTENING	1 cup (7 ounces)
FLOUR	2 cups (8 ounces)
MILK, hot	1½ gallons
CHICKEN, cooked, diced	3 cups (12 ounces)

Procedure

1. Combine soup base, water and vegetables. Simmer until vegetables are just tender.

2. Melt shortening; blend in flour. Gradually add hot milk. Cook and stir until slightly thickened.

3. Add vegetable mixture and chicken. Let stand over low heat to blend flavors.

Procedure

1. Dice bacon; fry slowly until crisp. Drain fat, reserving required amount.

2. Combine the bacon pieces, dry potato slices (direct from package), onions, salt, pepper and water. Cook until potatoes are soft, about 15 minutes.

3. Blend bacon fat and flour to make a smooth roux. Gradually add hot milk. Cook and stir until slightly thickened.

4. Add potato mixture.

5. Serve hot, garnished with parsley.

CHEESE DISHES

CHEESE, the versatile performer, appears in several sections of this book. As an ingredient, a topping or garnish, it imparts goodness and lends enchantment to dishes of many kinds. This section consists of entree recipes easily labeled as "Cheese Dishes" since their character depends so largely upon the kind and amount of cheese they contain.

Taken in its entirety, the cheese family is a sizable group. Some of its members are strictly for table service. Others lend themselves for cooking, melting graciously at the touch of heat.

In this country, Cheddar (or American) is a cooking favorite. And process American is a frequent choice because it obliges so readily when it comes to melting. Swiss, cottage, Mozzarella and Parmesan are other cheeses featured in this recipe selection. (With cooked Mozzarella, the chewy long strands are part of the fascination.)

A well-constructed cheese dish can easily carry off honors as a luncheon or supper item. Besides, it's easy to provide menu support with tart fruit juices, jaunty salads, crisp-tender green vegetables and fresh fruit or other desserts that offer a pleasing contrast in texture and taste.

CHIPPED BEEF AND CHEESE STRATA

Individual tomato aspic rings filled with a mixed, cooked vegetable salad complement this entree. A pineapple and walnut upside-down cake fits in nicely for dessert.

Yield: 36 portions

Ingredients

BREAD, white	72 slices
CHEESE, cheddar, shredded	2¼ pounds
CHIPPED BEEF	1½ pounds
BUTTER OR MARGARINE	4 ounces
EGGS, whole	2 quarts
MILK	1 gallon
ONION, grated	1 tablespoon
SALT	1 tablespoon
PEPPER	2 teaspoons
MUSTARD, dry	2 teaspoons

Procedure

1. Trim crusts from bread. Arrange 18 slices in bottom of each of two 12-inch by 20-inch by 2½-inch pans, fitting them close together.
2. Sprinkle cheese evenly over bread.
3. Frizzle chipped beef in butter. Distribute evenly over cheese in each pan.
4. Cover with remaining bread slices.
5. Beat eggs; combine with milk and seasonings.
6. Pour half the custard mixture over each pan.
7. Bake in a 325°F. oven 1¼ hours or until light and golden brown.

COTTAGE CHEESE PANCAKES

Pork sausages go well with these cherry-sauced cakes.

Yield: 4¼ gallons batter; 100 portions, 3 cakes each

Ingredients

EGGS, whole	10 pounds
FLOUR	3¾ pounds
SALT	4½ tablespoons
BAKING POWDER	2 tablespoons
SHORTENING, melted	4½ cups
COTTAGE CHEESE, large curd	18 pounds
CHERRIES, sour red, frozen, thawed	10 pounds
CORNSTARCH	2 ounces

CHEESE-HAM SOUFFLE

Garnish with broiled peach halves and offer an old-fashioned jelly roll for dessert.

Yield: 48 portions

Ingredients

EGG YOLKS	2 cups (1 pound)
MILK	2½ quarts
BREAD CUBES, ½-inch, soft	1 pound, 14 ounces
PROCESS CHEESE, grated	3 pounds
HAM, cooked, ground	5 pounds
GREEN PEPPER, chopped	1 cup (4 ounces)
PARSLEY, chopped	½ cup (1 ounce)
ONION, finely chopped	½ cup (2¼ ounces)
PAPRIKA	1½ teaspoons
CREAM OF TARTAR	2 teaspoons
EGG WHITES	3 cups (1½ pounds)

Procedure

1. Beat egg yolks. Add milk, bread cubes, cheese, ham, green pepper, parsley, onion and paprika.

2. Add cream of tartar to egg whites. Beat until stiff but not dry. Carefully fold into cheese mixture.

3. Turn mixture into two greased 12-inch by 20-inch by 2½-inch baking pans.

4. Bake in a 300°F. oven 1 hour or until knife inserted in center comes out clean. Serve at once.

▼   ▼

Procedure

1. Beat eggs until light.

2. Sift together flour, salt and baking powder.

3. Add dry ingredients and shortening to eggs; blend thoroughly.

4. Fold in cottage cheese; do not overmix. (Cheese should show as lumps in the cakes.)

5. Drain juice from cherries; blend with cornstarch. Cook until clear. Add cherries; heat.

6. Bake pancakes on hot griddle using a 2-ounce ladle to portion batter.

7. Serve pancakes with hot cherry sauce.

PIZZA

Constructed with a substantial topping, a wedge of pizza can become the focal point of a luncheon or supper meal that starts with cream of tomato soup and ends with a fruit cup made of fresh and canned fruit.

Yield: 8 10-inch pizzas

Ingredients

DOUGH

YEAST, compressed or active dry	2/3 ounces
WATER, (117°F.)	2-1/2 cups
COOKING OIL	1/4 cup
FLOUR	2 pounds
SALT	1-1/2 teaspoons

SAUCE

TOMATO PASTE	1-1/2 quarts
WATER, hot	2 cups
OREGANO	4 teaspoons
SALT	2 teaspoons
PEPPER	1 teaspoon

TOPPING

MOZZARELLA CHEESE, thinly sliced	1 pound
PARMESAN CHEESE, grated	3 ounces

Procedure to Make Dough

1. Dissolve yeast in warm water; add oil, flour and salt. Mix thoroughly. Knead for about 15 minutes or until smooth and elastic.

2. Place in greased bowl; brush with oil and let rise until double in bulk, about 2 hours.

3. Divide dough into 8 pieces; roll to fit 10-inch pans. Brush with oil.

4. Stack shells in refrigerator until ready to bake.

To Make Sauce

Combine ingredients, stirring to mix.

To Assemble Pizzas

1. Spread 1 cup sauce over each unbaked pizza shell.

2. Arrange 2 ounces mozzarella cheese over sauce in each shell. Add other toppings* as desired.

3. Sprinkle with Parmesan. Bake in a 500°F. oven 10 to 12 minutes, or until crust is brown. Serve at once.

*Suggested Toppings:

1. Thinly sliced ham, mushrooms and chopped green onions. 2. Tuna, sliced ripe olives and chopped parsley. 3. Anchovies. 4. Cooked pork sausage. 5. Pepperoni. 6. Whole ripe olives.

American Dairy Association

TOMATO-ONION RAREBIT

Celery hearts, olives and potato chips make nice go-alongs.

Yield: 24 portions

Ingredients

MARGARINE	4 ounces
CHEESE, sharp, cheddar, shredded	6 pounds
SALT	1 tablespoon
DRY MUSTARD	2 tablespoons
CAYENNE	dash
CREAM, light	1½ quarts
EGGS, well beaten	12
ONIONS, sweet, thinly sliced	2 quarts
MARGARINE	2 ounces
TOMATO SLICES, thick	24
MARGARINE	2 ounces
TOAST, buttered, trimmed	24 slices

Procedure

1. Melt margarine in a double boiler or in a heavy saucepan over low heat.

2. Add cheese; stir until melted.

3. Add salt, dry mustard, cayenne and the light cream, stirring constantly and keeping over low heat.

4. Add well beaten eggs to cheese mixture gradually. Do not let boil.

5. Saute onions in margarine until tender.

6. Grill the tomatoes in remaining margarine.

7. To serve arrange onions on buttered toast; top with a tomato slice; cover with rarebit sauce.

COTTAGE CHEESE FONDUE
Present with a grilled tomato half and buttered green peas.

Yield: 48 portions

Ingredients

BUTTER OR MARGARINE	¾ pound
SALT	2 tablespoons
PEPPER	½ teaspoon
FLOUR	6 ounces
MILK	1½ quarts
COTTAGE CHEESE, creamed	6 pounds
EGG YOLKS, lightly beaten	4 teaspoons
DRY MINCED ONION	15 ounces
BREAD CUBES, soft, ½-inch	1 pound
CREAM OF TARTAR	2 teaspoons
EGG WHITES	1½ pounds

Procedure

1. Melt butter in a 2 gallon saucepan. Blend in salt, pepper and flour. Add milk; cook, stirring constantly, until thick.

2. Stir in cottage cheese and beaten egg yolks. Continue cooking slowly until thoroughly heated, but do no boil. Remove from heat.

3. Add onion and bread cubes.

4. Add cream of tartar to egg whites; beat until stiff, but not dry. Fold carefully into cheese mixture.

5. Grease bottom of two 12-inch by 20-inch by 2½-inch baking pans. Pour mixture into pans.

6. Bake in a 300°F. oven for 1 hour, or until a knife inserted into center comes out clean. Serve immediately.

QUICHE LORRAINE

Serve with a leafy green salad, and for dessert, suggest a whole ripe pear or applesauce a la mode.

Yield: 8 9-inch pies

Ingredients

PASTRY PIE SHELLS, 9-inch, unbaked	8
BACON, sliced	2 pounds
EGGS, slightly beaten	2½ pounds
MILK	2 quarts
CREAM, light	2 quarts
SALT	2 tablespoons
PEPPER white	½ teaspoon
CAYENNE	½ teaspoon
CHEESE, Swiss, grated	2 pounds

Procedure

1. Bake pie shells in a 400°F. oven for 8 minutes only.
2. Fry bacon until crisp. Drain; crumble.
3. Combine eggs, milk, cream and seasonings.
4. Sprinkle bacon and cheese in partially baked pastry shells.
5. Pour in egg mixture allowing 2½ cups per pie.
6. Bake in a 400°F. oven 30 minutes or until knife inserted one inch from edge comes out clean.
6. Let set 15 minutes before serving.

BAKED CHEESE STRATA
Try garnishing portions with cranberry sauce or currant jelly.

Yield: 45 portions

Ingredients

BREAD, day-old	90 slices
PROCESS CHEESE, 1-ounce slices	45 slices
WHOLE EGG SOLIDS	4-1/2 cups
NONFAT DRY MILK	1-1/2 quarts
WATER	7-1/8 quarts
ONION, finely chopped	3 tablespoons
SALT	3 tablespoons
MUSTARD, dry	1 tablespoon
PAPRIKA	1 tablespoon

Procedure

1. Trim crusts from bread.

2. Arrange 15 slices in bottom of each of 3 greased 12-inch by 20-inch by 2½-inch baking pans, fitting them close together.

3. Place a slice of cheese on each slice of bread; cover with remaining bread slices.

4. Sift eggs and milk over water in a 4-gallon mixing bowl. Beat with wire whip until smooth.

5. Add onion, salt and mustard; blend well.

6. Pour 1/3 of the egg mixture over the cheese sandwiches in each pan. Sprinkle with paprika.

7. Bake in a 350°F. oven 1 hour or until puffed and golden brown.

Casserole of Baked Beans, Apples and Frankfurters,
recipe, p. 34

Processed Apples Institute, Inc.

VEGETABLE ENTREES

THIS SECTION features entrees with vegetables in a leading role. Some dishes are homey in nature, others sophisticated. But even the most familiar items flaunt an imaginative new twist.

Bean dishes—with tasty additions of frankfurters, smoked ham, shredded cheese or surprising bits of fruit—dot the list. An old fashioned baked corn custard takes on a new dimension from fresh corn, a subtle hint of mustard and cheddar cheese.

For more of the unusual, vegetables combine in casseroles, croquettes, a quiche and souffle. And potatoes fashion the shell for an excitingly different main-dish pie.

BAKED BEANS WITH APRICOTS

Present with iceberg lettuce hearts topped with Russian dressing and mention Key Lime Pie as a thought for dessert.

Yield: 24 portions

Ingredients

APRICOTS, dried, finely chopped	1 pound
PORK SAUSAGE LINKS	1½ pounds
BAKED BEANS IN TOMATO SAUCE	2 54-ounce cans
BROWN SUGAR, firmly packed	½ cup

Procedure

1. Cover apricots with boiling water; allow to stand 5 minutes. Drain.
2. Brown the sausages; cut into half-inch pieces.
3. Combine all the ingredients. Turn into a baking pan; bake in a 375°F. oven for 35 minutes or until thoroughly heated.

VEGETABLE-STUFFED GREEN PEPPERS WITH TONGUE

Round out the menu with a bibb lettuce salad and bananas baked with brown sugar and rum.

Yield: 16 portions

Ingredients

GREEN PEPPERS	8 whole
ONIONS, chopped	4 ounces
MUSHROOM PIECES, canned	10 ounces
BUTTER or MARGARINE	4 ounces
RICE, cooked	2 cups
SALT	2 teaspoons
PIMIENTO, chopped	2 ounces
PEAS, canned, drained	1 pound
TONGUE, hot, sliced	3 pounds

Procedure

1. Cut each pepper in half; remove seeds and membrane. Steam or parboil 5 minutes; drain.
2. Saute onion and mushrooms in butter until onions are tender but not brown. Add rice, salt, pimiento and peas.
3. Fill green pepper shells with rice mixture. Place in a shallow baking pan. Pour a small amount of hot water around peppers.
4. Bake in a 350°F. oven 35 to 40 minutes or until peppers are tender.
5. Serve with hot sliced tongue.

TROPICAL BEANS AND FRANKS

An easily assembled main-dish. Add assorted relishes and ice cream, voila, a meal!

Yield: 48 portions

Ingredients

FRANKFURTERS	6 pounds
PINEAPPLE TIDBITS, drained	1 No. 10 can
SUGAR, light brown	¼ cup
BUTTER or MARGARINE	6 ounces
BEANS IN TOMATO SAUCE	2 54-ounce cans
MUSTARD, prepared	¼ cup
CLOVES, ground	1 teaspoon

Procedure

1. Cut each frankfurter into 5 pieces.
2. Saute frankfurters, pineapple and sugar in butter until excess juice from pineapple has evaporated.
3. Combine beans, mustard and cloves; add frankfurters and pineapple. Turn into two 18-inch by 12-inch by 2-inch baking pans.
4. Bake in a 375°F. oven 20 minutes or until thoroughly hot.

APPLESAUCE SWEET POTATOES

Offer with Canadian bacon and a fresh asparagus salad with Floating Island in the offing for dessert.

Yield: Approx. 28 portions

Ingredients

SWEET POTATOES, drained	1 No. 10 can
SALT	1 teaspoon
APPLESAUCE	1 quart
SUGAR, brown	9 ounces
CINNAMON	2 teaspoons
WALNUTS, chopped	1 cup
BUTTER or MARGARINE, melted	4 ounces

Procedure

1. Put drained sweet potatoes into a 12-inch by 18-inch by 2-inch baking pan. Sprinkle with salt.
2. Spoon applesauce over top.
3. Combine brown sugar, cinnamon and nuts; sprinkle over top. Drizzle with melted butter.
4. Bake in a 375°F. oven 45 minutes.

BAKED BEANS, IDAHO STYLE

List on the menu with slices of steamed brown bread and cole slaw.

Yield: 50 8-ounce portions

Ingredients

GREAT NORTHERN BEANS	7 pounds
WATER	as needed
WHOLE ONIONS, stuck with cloves	4
BAY LEAVES	4
GARLIC CLOVES	4
BUTTER	2 ounces
SALT PORK, cubed	2 pounds
ONIONS, chopped	1½ cups
SUGAR, brown	8 ounces
MUSTARD, dry	1 ounce
SALT	2 ounces
MOLASSES, dark	2 cups
CATSUP	2 cups
WORCESTERSHIRE SAUCE	1 tablespoon
LIQUID FROM BEANS	3 quarts
WATER	as needed

Procedure

1. Wash beans. Soak overnight in water to cover.

2. Add onions, bay leaves, garlic and butter. Bring to boiling. Reduce heat; cover and simmer about 2 hours or until skins start to roll off.

3. Remove onions and bay leaves. Drain beans, reserving liquid.

4. Place beans in baking pans. Add cubed salt pork and chopped onions; distribute well among beans.

5. Combine remaining ingredients, except water. Pour over beans in pans. Add water as needed to fill pans.

6. Cover; bake in a 250°F. oven 10 to 12 hours or overnight. (If small pots or casseroles are used, bake 7 to 8 hours). Remove covers for last hour or two of baking to brown beans.

PIZZA POTATO PIE

Pillsbury Food Service Div.

Teams easily with a molded raw vegetable salad and warm apple crisp a la mode.

Yield: One 18-inch by 26-inch pan (48 3-inch squares) or 5 9-inch pie pans.

Ingredients

CRUST

DEHYDRATED POTATO CUBES	1¼ pounds (6½ cups)
EGGS, unbeaten	4
SALT	2 teaspoons
OREGANO	1 teaspoon
ONION SALT	1¼ teaspoons

FILLING

GROUND BEEF	5 pounds
ONIONS, diced	1 cup
TOMATO JUICE, concentrated	1 36-ounce can
WATER	3 cups
MUSHROOMS, canned	1 pound
CHEESE, CHEDDAR, grated	3 cups (12 ounces)

Procedure

CRUST

1. Prepare dehydrated potato cubes according to label directions. Drain. (Or, use 1½ quarts, hot, cooked, cubed potatoes.)

2. Stir in eggs and seasonings.

3. Pat into well-greased 18-inch by 26-inch sheet pan. Or, into well-greased 9-inch pie pans, allowing 2 cups potato mixture per pan.

4. Bake in a 450°F. oven 15 minutes.

FILLING

1. Brown meat and onions.

2. Add concentrated tomato juice, water and mushrooms.

3. Heat; spread on crust (for 9-inch pie pans, allow 2½ cups filling per pan). Top with cheese.

4. Bake in a 450°F. oven 10 to 15 minutes or until cheese melts. Let rest in pan 15 minutes before cutting and serving.

YAM AND PEANUT CROQUETTES

Serve with crisp bacon strips, a grapefruit and avocado salad and a wedge of cheese cake with cherry glaze.

Yield: 50 (No. 12 scoop)

Ingredients

YAMS, cooked, mashed	10 pounds
OR	
CANNED YAMS, mashed	1-1/2 No. 10 cans
EGG YOLKS, beaten	16
CREAM	1 cup
NUTMEG	2 teaspoons
SUGAR	1/3 cup
SALT	2 teaspoons
PEANUTS, salted, chopped	1-1/2 pounds
EGGS, beaten	6
MILK	1 cup
CORN FLAKES, crushed	1-1/2 pounds

Procedure

1. Place mashed yams in mixer bowl. Add egg yolks and cream; mix well.
2. Add nutmeg, sugar, salt and chopped peanuts; mix well.
3. Dip with a No. 12 scoop; shape into croquettes. Chill.
4. Beat eggs and milk together. Dip croquettes in mixture; roll in crumbs.
5. Fry in deep fat at 375°F. for 3 to 4 minutes.

CREOLE LIMA BEANS ══════════════════

Try billing with buttered leaf spinach and apricot pie.

Yield: 25 portions

Ingredients

DRIED LIMA BEANS	2½ pounds
WATER, cold	as needed
ONIONS, chopped	1¼ cups
BUTTER or MARGARINE	4 ounces
CHILI POWDER	1½ tablespoons
SALT	2 tablespoons
TOMATOES, canned	2 quarts
CHEESE, AMERICAN PROCESS, shredded	2 pounds

RIPE OLIVE ONION TARTS

Serve with sauteed chicken livers and broiled cherry tomatoes. Have fresh pineapple slices for dessert.

Yield: 24 4-inch tarts

Ingredients

PIE PASTRY DOUGH	2 pounds
ONIONS, thinly sliced	2¼ pounds
BUTTER or MARGARINE	½ pound
FLOUR	1½ ounces (6 tablespoons)
HALF AND HALF	1 quart
EGGS, slightly beaten	10 large
SALT	1 tablespoon
PEPPER, white	¼ teaspoon
NUTMEG	¼ teaspoon
CAYENNE	dash
RIPE OLIVE HALVES	14 ounces (3½ cups)

Procedure

1. Roll out pastry; line 24 4-inch quiche pans, about 1 inch deep.
2. Cook onions slowly in butter until soft but not browned.
3. Blend in flour. Add half and half; cook and stir until mixture boils and thickens.
4. Cool slightly; stir in eggs. Blend in seasonings and ripe olives.
5. Portion into pastry lined pans, allowing about 4 ounces per pan. Set on baking sheet.
6. Bake in a 375°F. oven about 30 minutes, until pastry is browned and filling set.

Procedure

1. Wash beans. Cover with cold water; let stand 2 hours. Simmer until tender. Drain.
2. Saute onion in butter until tender but not brown. Add chili powder, salt and tomatoes; mix well.
3. Combine beans and tomato mixture. Fill individual casseroles half full. Sprinkle with half the cheese. Fill with remaining beans.
4. Bake in a 350°F. oven 30 minutes. Sprinkle with remaining cheese. Continue baking until cheese melts.

CASSEROLE OF BAKED BEANS,
APPLES AND FRANKFURTERS

Add carrot sticks and celery hearts to the plate and put whipped gelatin with custard sauce on for dessert.

Yield: 25 portions

Ingredients

BAKED BEANS, New England style	1 No. 10 can
APPLE SLICES	1 No. 10 can
CHILI SAUCE or CATSUP	1 cup
ONION, finely chopped	1 cup
SUGAR, light brown	1 cup (packed)
WORCESTERSHIRE SAUCE	¼ cup
FRANKFURTERS	5 pounds

Procedure

1. Combine baked beans, apple slices, chili sauce, onion, brown sugar and Worcestershire sauce.
2. Divide mixture into 25 individual casseroles.
3. Cut each frankfurter into two pieces; place 3 halves on top of each casserole.
4. Bake in a 350°F. oven about 30 minutes, until slightly browned on top.

LIMA-HAM-PIMIENTO SCALLOP

Add a pineapple and cottage cheese salad, whole wheat rolls and lemon sherbet drizzled with brandy to complete the menu.

Yield: 50 portions

Ingredients

BABY LIMA BEANS, drained	1 No. 10 can
HAM, cooked, cubed	6 pounds
PIMIENTOS, chopped	1 quart
MUSHROOMS, sliced (canned)	2 cups
PARSLEY, minced	1 cup
CREAM SAUCE, medium	1 gallon
BUTTERED CRUMBS	1 quart

Procedure

1. Add lima beans, ham, pimientos, mushrooms and parsley to cream sauce.
2. Turn into baking pans or individual casseroles. Top with crumbs.
3. Bake in a 350°F. oven 30 to 35 minutes.

TOMATO CHEESE FONDUE

This convivial dish can become a conversation piece as a feature on a festive buffet.

Yield: 2¼ quarts 48 portions

Ingredients

CREAM OF TOMATO SOUP, condensed	1 50 or 51 ounce can
PROCESS CHEESE, grated	2 pounds
HOT PEPPER SAUCE	½ teaspoon
MUSTARD, dry	1½ teaspoons
BITTERS	½ teaspoon
FRENCH BREAD	1 1-pound loaf

Procedure

1. Heat undiluted soup slowly in a 3-quart saucepan. Do not boil.

2. Gradually add cheese; stir until all the cheese is melted. Blend in seasonings.

3. Pour into a chafing dish over a water bath. Keep fondue hot during service.

4. Cut bread in 1-inch chunks, each having at least one side of crust. Toast if desired.

5. To serve: using a tooth pick or fork, each person dips a bread cube into hot tomato fondue, twists it around and eats it immediately.

SCALLOPED POTATOES WITH CHEESE

Present with a skewer of Vienna sausages, ham squares and cherry tomatoes and offer walnut prune whip for dessert.

Yield: 24 portions

Ingredients

POTATOES, white, raw, cut in ½-in. dice	1 gallon (6 pounds)
CREAM OF CHICKEN SOUP, condensed	1 50-ounce can
MILK	1¼ to 1½ cups
CHEESE, cheddar, shredded	3 cups (12 ounces)
BREAD CRUMBS, buttered	1 cup

Procedure

1. Boil or steam potatoes; drain, if necessary.

2. Combine soup and milk; heat to simmer. Add cheese, stirring until melted.

3. Combine sauce and potatoes. Turn into a 12-inch by 18-inch by 2-inch baking pan. Sprinkle with buttered crumbs.

4. Bake in a 400°F. oven 45 minutes or until mixture is thoroughly hot and surface is golden.

VEGETABLE AND BACON BAKE

Companionable items include a tomato aspic salad and peanut butter cup custard with chocolate sauce.

Yield: 24 portions

Ingredients

SALT	1 tablespoon
WATER, boiling	2 quarts
INSTANT POTATOES,sliced	9 ounces
BACON	1½ pounds
CARROTS, thinly sliced, cooked	3 cups
GREEN BEANS, cooked	1½ quarts
ONIONS, finely chopped	15 ounces
MILK, liquid nonfat dry*	3 quarts
BACON FAT	1¼ cups
FLOUR	6 ounces
CHEESE, CHEDDAR, grated	12 ounces
SALT	1 tablespoon
PEPPER	¾ teaspoon
BUTTER or MARGARINE, melted	¼ cup
BREAD CRUMBS, fine dry	3 ounces

Procedure

1. Add salt to boiling water. Add instant potatoes. Simmer, covered 15 minutes or until potatoes are tender. (Do not overcook.) Drain well.

2. Cook bacon crisp. Drain, reserving fat. Crumble bacon.

3. Combine potatoes, bacon, carrots, green beans and onions.

4. Heat milk. Prepare a roux of bacon fat and flour. Add to hot milk, stirring constantly with a wire whip. Cook and stir until thickened and smooth.

5. Remove sauce from heat; add cheese, salt and pepper.

6. Combine cheese sauce and vegetable mixture. Pour into a 20-inch by 12-inch by 2½-inch baking pan.

7. Toss crumbs with melted butter. Sprinkle on top of pan; bake in a 350°F. oven 30 to 40 minutes.

*Reconstituted according to label directions.

VEGETABLE SOUFFLE

Try teaming with a jellied Waldorf salad and oatmeal cookies. And if you would like to dress the souffle with a companionable sauce, thin additional mushroom soup with light cream and add a dash of lemon juice.

Yield: 48 portions

Ingredients

CONDENSED MUSHROOM SOUP	1 50 or 51 ounce can
PROCESS CHEESE, grated	1½ pounds
EGG YOLKS	1 pound
MIXED VEGETABLES, frozen	3 pounds, 12 ounces
WORCESTERSHIRE SAUCE	1 teaspoon
CURRY POWDER (optional)	1½ teaspoons
SALT	1½ teaspoons
PEPPER	½ teaspoon
BREAD CUBES, soft, ½-inch	1¼ pounds
CREAM OF TARTAR	2 teaspoons
EGG WHITES	1½ pounds

Procedure

1. Heat undiluted mushroom soup in a 1 gallon saucepan. Blend in grated cheese; stir until smooth and cheese is melted. Remove from heat.

2. Beat egg yolks until thick and lemon colored; add gradually to soup mixture. Cook over low heat, stirring constantly until thick, but do not boil.

3. Place frozen vegetables in a 3 gallon bowl. Combine with hot sauce and seasonings.

4. Fold bread cubes into sauce.

5. Add cream of tartar to egg whites; beat until stiff but not dry. Fold carefully into sauce mixture.

6. Grease bottoms of two 12-inch by 20-inch by 2½-inch pans. Pour mixture into pans.

7. Bake in a 300°F. oven for 1 hour, or until knife inserted into center comes out clean. Serve immediately.

FRESH MUSHROOM QUICHE

A salad of brittle-crisp romaine leaves, a glass of red wine and freshly baked bread form good partnerships with this quiche.

Yield: 4 9-inch quiche

Ingredients

BACON, sliced	1 pound
BACON FAT	3/4 cup
ONION, finely chopped	1-1/3 cups
MUSHROOMS, coarsely chopped	2 pounds
FLOUR	1/4 cup
EGGS, lightly beaten	16
CREAM, heavy	1 quart
MILK	3 cups
SALT	2 teaspoons
BLACK PEPPER, ground	1/2 teaspoon
NUTMEG, ground	3/4 teaspoon
PASTRY SHELLS, 9-inch, unbaked	4
GRUYERE CHEESE, grated	1 pound
MUSHROOM CAPS, whole, broiled	as needed

Procedure

1. Cook bacon until crisp. Drain. Crumble. Measure required amount of bacon fat.

2. Saute onion in bacon fat until limp. Add chopped mushrooms. Saute until tender, adding more bacon fat, if necessary. Blend in flour. Cool mixture a few minutes.

3. Combine eggs, cream, milk and seasonings.

4. Sprinkle crumbled bacon over bottom of pastry shells. Top with grated cheese. Spread with mushroom mixture. Pour egg mixture over all.

5. Bake in 425°F. oven 15 minutes. Reduce heat to 300°F.; bake 40 minutes longer or until custard is set.

6. Serve warm, garnished with broiled mushroom caps.

FRESH CORN AND CHEDDAR PUDDING

Feature with cold sliced baked ham and a wedge of melon topped with fruit.

Yield: 24 portions

Ingredients

MUSTARD, powdered	1 tablespoon
WATER	1 tablespoon
BUTTER or MARGARINE	8 ounces
FLOUR	4 ounces (1 cup)
MILK	1½ quarts
CHEDDAR CHEESE, shredded	1½ pounds
CORN, cut-off-the-cob	1½ quarts
BREAD CRUMBS, soft	1 quart
SALT	1½ tablespoons
SUGAR	2 teaspoons
BLACK PEPPER, ground	1 teaspoon
EGGS, beaten	16

Procedure

1. Combine mustard and water; let stand 10 minutes for flavor to develop.

2. Melt butter; blend in flour.

3. Gradually stir in milk; cook and stir over low heat until thickened and smooth.

4. Remove from heat. Add mustard and remaining ingredients; mix well.

5. Turn into buttered baking pans or individual casseroles. Place in a pan of hot water. Bake in a 325°F. oven 1 hour, 15 minutes or until knife inserted in center comes out clean.

American Dairy Association

EGG DISHES

THERE MAY be (as it's been said) more than a thousand ways to fix an egg. Without quibbling over figures, we all know that plain and fancy egg dishes are welcome from breakfast time on. And, it's anyone's guess as to the number that can provide a perfectly wonderful answer for a luncheon or supper menu.

There are, of course, scrambled eggs with sundry additions and omelets with all manner of savory fillings. The open-face Italian omelet, known as the frittata is another version with its own special merits.

Hard-cooked eggs combine in casserole dishes of numerous kinds. And provide the basis for Egg Croquettes (lightly seasoned with curry); Eggs Supreme a la Creme (presented on baked noodle squares); and Goldenrod Eggs in Pimiento Petal shells—all of these only hint of the exciting possibilities you'll find on the pages ahead.

EGGS SUPREME A LA CREME

Garnish with wedges of tomato and parsley or cress. For dessert—an ice cream pie in a coconut crust.

Yield: 48 portions

Ingredients

WHITE SAUCE, medium (prepared with half milk, half chicken broth)	1 gallon
EGGS, hard-cooked, sliced	36
PEAS, canned, drained	1½ quarts
PIMIENTO	½ cup
DILL WEED	1½ teaspoons

Procedure

1. Combine ingredients; heat through.
2. Serve over baked noodle squares.

BAKED NOODLE SQUARES

Yield: 48 portions

Ingredients

NOODLES, medium width	2 pounds
CHEESE, American process (sharp) shredded	3 pounds
BREAD CRUMBS, dry	8 ounces
ONION, chopped	12 ounces
MUSHROOMS, canned, drained, chopped	12 ounces
GREEN PEPPER, chopped	5 ounces
EGGS, beaten	18
MILK	3 quarts
SALT	3 tablespoons
PEPPER	1 teaspoon

Procedure

1. Cook noodles in boiling salted water. Drain; divide equally into two 12-inch by 20-inch by 2-inch pans.
2. Sprinkle half of cheese, bread crumbs, onion, mushrooms and green pepper over each pan of noodles.
3. Combine eggs, milk and seasonings. Pour half of mixture over each pan of noodles; mix thoroughly.
4. Bake in a 350°F. oven 1½ hours.
5. Cut each pan into 24 squares.

EGG CROQUETTES

This is a dish that teams well with a thin parsley cream sauce and cut green beans. It is also in good company with escalloped potatoes (which can rule out the need for the creamy sauce).

Yield: 40 croquettes

Ingredients

ONIONS, finely chopped	1/3 cup
GREEN PEPPERS, finely chopped	1/3 cup
MILK	1 quart
SHORTENING	3/4 cup
FLOUR	1½ cups
SALT	1½ tablespoons
PEPPER, black	1/4 teaspoon
WORCESTERSHIRE SAUCE	1/3 cup
EGGS, hard-cooked	36
CORN FLAKE CRUMBS	3 cups
CURRY POWDER	1 tablespoon
EGGS, slightly beaten	6

Procedure

1. Combine onions, green pepper and milk; heat.
2. Melt shortening in sauce pot or steam jacketed kettle. Blend in flour. Add hot milk mixture; cook and stir until mixture thickens.
3. Add salt, pepper and Worcestershire sauce. Remove from heat.
4. Chop eggs medium fine. Fold into sauce. Chill mixture several hours or overnight.
5. Portion with a No. 20 scoop; shape into croquettes, being careful to avoid cracks or holes.
6. Mix cornflake crumbs with curry powder.
7. Dip each croquette into beaten egg; roll in seasoned crumbs. Refrigerate at least two hours.
8. Fry in deep fat at 350°F. until golden brown.

VILLAGE HAM 'N EGGS

Add a spinach and grapefruit salad and offer ice cream with blonde brownies for dessert.

Yield: 48 portions

Ingredients

HAM, cooked	5 pounds
BUTTER or MARGARINE	12 ounces
FLOUR	2 cups
MILK, heated	1 gallon
CHEESE, process cheddar, grated	1½ pounds
SALT	2 teaspoons
PEPPER	1 teaspoon
PIMIENTO, diced	¾ cup
EGGS, hard-cooked, diced	24
ENGLISH MUFFINS, split, toasted	48

Procedure

1. Cut ham in julienne strips.
2. Melt butter; blend in flour.
3. Add hot milk and grated cheese. Cook and stir over medium heat until sauce is thick and smooth.
4. Add seasonings, pimiento, ham and eggs.
5. Serve hot over toasted muffins.

TOMATO-EGG SCRAMBLE

Accompany with a salad of diced lettuce hearts tossed with cucumber and celery. And for dessert, suggest squares of warm gingerbread with lemon sauce.

Yield: 48 portions

Ingredients

CREAM OF TOMATO SOUP, condensed	2 50 or 51-ounce cans
PROCESS AMERICAN CHEESE, grated	3 pounds
EGGS, whole	1 gallon
SALT	1½ tablespoons
MILK	3 cups
ENRICHED BREAD TOAST, buttered	48 slices
BACON, cooked (optional)	96 slices
PARSLEY SPRIGS	48

GOLDENROD EGGS IN PIMIENTO PETAL SHELLS

As a menu suggestion, serve with green lima beans, coleslaw and a pineapple and orange ambrosia.

Yield: 24

Ingredients

WHITE SAUCE, medium, hot	1¼ quarts
CAYENNE PEPPER	dash
CREAM, heavy, slightly beaten	1 cup
EGGS, hard-cooked	20
PIMIENTOS, whole	4 7-ounce cans
TART SHELLS (pastry) baked	24

Procedure

1. Combine white sauce, cayenne and cream.

2. Cut the hard-cooked eggs into halves. Remove the yolks from one-fourth of the eggs; reserve for garnish.

3. Cut remainder of eggs into pieces; fold into sauce. Heat thoroughly. Check seasoning; add salt and white pepper if needed.

4. Cut petal shaped pieces from pimientos. Place around edges of baked shells, allowing 3 to 4 pieces of pimiento per shell.

5. Press reserved yolks through a sieve.

6. Fill shells with hot egg mixture. Garnish with sieved yolks.

Procedure

1. Combine undiluted soup and grated cheese in top of a double boiler. Place over boiling water; heat, stirring occasionally, until cheese melts and blends evenly into soup.

2. Beat eggs slightly; add salt and milk; blend. Scramble just before serving time.

3. For each portion, ladle 1/3 cup of the tomato-cheese sauce over a No. 8 scoop of scrambled eggs. Cut a slice of buttered toast across diagonally. Arrange on the plate with two bacon strips, if desired. Garnish with parsley.

MUSHROOM OMELET

*A fluffy baked omelet to cut into squares and top with a savory mush-
room sauce.*

Yield: 24 portions

Ingredients

OMELET

EGG YOLKS, beaten	48 (1 quart)
MILK	1½ cups
CORNSTARCH	½ cup
BUTTER, melted	¾ pound
SALT	2 to 3 teaspoons
EGG WHITES	48 (1½ quarts)
SAUCE	
MUSHROOMS, sliced	1½ pounds
BUTTER	6 ounces
TOMATO SAUCE	1½ quarts
CHEESE, processed cheddar	1½ pounds

Procedure

1. Combine egg yolks, milk, cornstarch, butter and salt.

2. Beat egg whites until they form stiff glossy peaks. Fold into yolk
mixture.

3. Pour into 12-inch x 20-inch x 2-inch pan. Bake in a 325°F. oven
1 hour or until done.

To Make Sauce:

4. Saute mushrooms in butter. Stir in tomato sauce and cheese.
Heat and stir until cheese melts and mixture is blended.

To Serve:

5. Cut omelet in 3-inch squares. Serve with 1/3 cup sauce.

American Dairy Association

EGGS FLORENTINE

An easy-to-prepare variation of the classic version which calls for poached eggs.

Yield: 15 portions

Ingredients

SPINACH, frozen	1 pound, 14 ounces
SALT	1 tablespoon
CREAM, light	¼ cup
MARGARINE	2 tablespoons
CHEESE, SWISS, grated	¼ cup
EGGS, frozen whole eggs, thawed	2 pounds (1 quart)
MARGARINE	6 tablespoons
FLOUR	¼ cup
MILK	3 cups
CHEESE, SWISS, grated	1 cup (4 ounces)

Procedure

1. Cook spinach, drain well

2. Combine spinach, salt, light cream and first amount of margarine; toss to mix. Turn into a lightly greased 15-inch x 9-inch x 2-inch pan, spreading evenly. Sprinkle first amount of cheese over spinach.

3. Pour eggs evenly over spinach. Cover pan with foil.

4. Bake in a 350°F. oven 45 minutes or until egg is firm to touch.

5. Prepare a white sauce with remaining margarine, flour and milk. When sauce thickens, add remaining cheese; stir until melted.

6. Cut baked egg into 3-inch squares. Serve hot with 3 tablespoons cheese sauce over each square.

FRENCH TOAST WITH STRAWBERRY BUTTER
Feature with country sausage cakes and sherried grapefruit halves.

Yield: 20 portions

Ingredients

STRAWBERRIES, frozen, sliced	1 pound
SYRUP, reserved from strawberries	½ cup
BUTTER or MARGARINE, soft	6 ounces
SUGAR, confectioners'	3 tablespoons
EGGS, slightly beaten	5
SUGAR, granulated	1 tablespoon
VANILLA	¾ teaspoon
MILK	½ cup
BREAD, white day-old	40 slices
CORN FLAKE CRUMBS	2½ cups

Procedure

1. Drain strawberries. Measure required amount of syrup; set aside.

2. Whip butter until light and fluffy. Add confectioners' sugar gradually, beating thoroughly.

3. Heat strawberries (with remaining syrup) until slightly warm. Add to butter mixture gradually, beating thoroughly. Chill until ready to use.

4. Combine eggs, sugar and vanilla; beat well. Add milk and measured amount of strawberry syrup.

5. Dip bread slices in egg mixture; moisten thoroughly, turning once. Coat both sides with cornflake crumbs.

6. Brown bread slices in small amount of heated shortening. Serve at once with strawberry butter.

EGGS SCANDIA

Ripe olives make an attractive garnish for this entree that you can bill with a tomato juice appetizer and a pecan tart.

Yield: 2½ quarts sauce; 30 1/3-cup portions

Ingredients

MILK	2½ quarts
FLOUR	1¼ cups (5 ounces)
INSTANT MINCED ONION	½ cup
SALT	2 tablespoons
PEPPER	½ teaspoon
CURRY POWDER	1 teaspoon
DRY MUSTARD	½ teaspoon
BUTTER or MARGARINE	¼ pound
LEMON JUICE	¼ cup
WHOLE BLUE LAKE GREEN BEANS	1 No. 10 can
ENGLISH MUFFINS, CORNBREAD SQUARES or HOT BISCUITS	30
EGGS, hard-cooked, halved	30

Procedure

1. Combine 3 cups of milk with flour, stirring to a smooth paste. Stir into remaining milk.

2. Add onion, salt, pepper, curry powder, mustard and butter. Cook, stirring constantly, until mixture thickens and boils.

3. Remove from heat; stir in lemon juice.

4. Heat beans in liquid from can; drain.

5. Split muffins, cornbread or biscuit. Toast muffin or cornbread. Arrange two halves on each serving plate.

6. Spoon beans on one half, leave other half uncovered. Top beans with two pieces of egg. Ladle 1/3 cup sauce over eggs.

FRITTATA LOMBARDY

A tossed green salad and crusty dark bread are fine go-alongs for this Italian-style omelet.

Yield: 24 portions

Ingredients

ONIONS, sliced	12 ounces
GREEN PEPPE R, slivered	12 ounces
COOKING OIL	2 tablespoons
TOMATOES, fresh	3 pounds
TOMATO PUREE, canned	1 quart
SALT	4 teaspoons
OREGANO	1 teaspoon
RIPE OLIVES, canned, pitted, whole or cut in halves	12 ounces
EGGS	3 quarts
MILK	1 quart
SALT	2 tablespoons
HAM, slivered	1½ pounds

Procedure

1. Saute onions and green pepper in oil over low heat until transparent but not browned.

2. Scald tomatoes; peel; remove stem ends. Cut in halves crosswise; remove most of the seeds and juice. Dice seeded tomatoes; add to onions and peppers.

3. Add tomato puree, salt and oregano.

4. Cook until thickened, about 30 minutes, stirring occasionally. Add olives.

5. Beat eggs with milk and salt.

6. For each portion, saute 1 ounce ham; keep warm. Make omelet using 2/3 cup egg mixture in well buttered 8-inch omelet pan. When eggs are set, top with ham and 1/3 cup olive tomato sauce. Serve omelet open-face (without folding).

EGGS AGEMONO

This dish, which resembles Eggs Foo Yong, dictates that the vegetables should remain crisp. If desired, serve on a bed of rice with Chinese pea pods on the side.

Yield: 18 portions

Ingredients

CORNSTARCH	1/3 cup
SOY SAUCE	3 tablespoons
MOLASSES, dark	3 tablespoons
VINEGAR, cider	3 tablespoons
CHICKEN BROTH	1 quart
COOKED HAM, PORK or CHICKEN, cut in fine strips or	
SMALL WHOLE SHRIMP, cooked	2 cups
ONIONS, finely chopped	2 cups
CELERY, finely cut	2 cups
SALT	2 teaspoons
CORN FLAKE CRUMBS	1 cup
SOY SAUCE	2 tablespoons
EGGS, whole	35 (1¾ quarts)
VEGETABLE OIL	as needed

Procedure

1. Combine cornstarch, first amount of soy sauce, molasses and vinegar; stir until smooth.

2. Gradually stir in chicken broth; bring to boiling point, stirring constantly. Reduce heat; simmer 10 minutes or until sauce is thickened and clear. Keep hot.

3. Combine meat or shrimp, onions, celery, salt and cereal crumbs; toss lightly to mix.

4. Add remaining soy sauce to eggs; beat slightly. Combine eggs and meat mixture.

5. Heat a small amount of vegetable oil in frypan or on grill heated to 350°F.

6. Portion mixture into hot oil, using No. 24 scoop. Fry until lightly browned on each side, turning only once.

7. Ladle hot sauce over patties or present sauce separately.

DEVILED EGGS IN PIMIENTO SAUCE

Serve with broccoli spears and have chocolate layer cake for dessert.

Yield: 50 portions (3 halves)

Ingredients

EGGS, hard-cooked	75 (6-1/4 dozen)
SALT	2 tablespoons
MUSTARD, dry	1 tablespoon
PEPPER	1 teaspoon
PIMIENTO, minced	1/4 cup
MAYONNAISE	2 cups
CREAM	1/2 cup (about)
SAUCE	
BUTTER or MARGARINE	12 ounces
FLOUR	6 ounces
MILK, hot	2-1/2 quarts
SALT	1-1/3 tablespoons
PREPARED MUSTARD	1 tablespoon
DEHYDRATED ONION	1 teaspoon
EGG YOLKS	4 (3 ounces)
PIMIENTO, chopped	1 cup

Procedure

1. Peel eggs, cut in half lengthwise; remove yolks. Place whites on trays for easy filling.

2. Mash yolks, add remaining ingredients. Mix until smooth and creamy, using wire whip. Add more cream, if necessary to make a light, smooth mixture.

3. Put yolk mixture in pastry bag with plain tip; fill halves.

4. Cover; refrigerate until ready to combine with sauce.

To Make Sauce:

5. Make a white sauce of butter, flour and milk.

6. Mix seasonings with egg yolks. Add a small amount of white sauce; blend well. Stir egg yolk mixture into white sauce. Add chopped pimiento.

To Serve:

7. Keep filled eggs warm in steam unit. Place 3 egg halves on 1 slice buttered toast. Cover with a 2-ounce ladle of very hot sauce. Garnish with chopped parsley, if desired.

American Dairy Association

PASTA and RICE

MENU MAKERS who find themselves pressed for attractive yet thrifty luncheon and supper ideas will welcome the exciting possibilities (and favorable advantages) of the different types of entrees fashioned with rice or pasta.

Bland in themselves, rice and the various pasta products—macaroni, spaghetti and noodles—combine easily with meat, fish, shellfish, poultry and cheese. And at the same time permit sprightly additions of seasonings, flavorful sauces and other savory trimmings.

The scope takes in pancakes, croquettes and quiche as well as casserole-type dishes that range from prestigious Tetrazzini dishes to the more familiar macaroni and cheese.

Rice and pasta have the happy faculty of making costlier ingredients go a long way. And they are, by good fortune, flexible too. Simply changing the kind or shape of the pasta can change the character and bring new attention to the dish. For example, substituting green noodles for the regular style immediately steps up the importance of an item. And, using shell macaroni in a seafood and pasta offering changes the spirit, adds a new dimension.

And for one more plus to keep in mind: many casserole combinations mellow and blend as they cook. Most of them hold well, improve their flavors as they wait.

NOODLE QUICHE
Garnish portions with radishes, cucumber pickles and cress.

Yield: 4 9-inch (24 portions)

Ingredients

EGG NOODLES, fine	1 pound
ONIONS, finely chopped	2 cups
BUTTER or MARGARINE	2 ounces
EGGS, beaten	8
CREAM, light	1½ quarts
SALT	½ teaspoon
PEPPER	¼ teaspoon
DILL WEED	4 teaspoons
PASTRY PIE SHELLS, 9-inch, unbaked	4
CHEESE, sharp Cheddar or Swiss, grated	½ pound

Procedure

1. Cook noodles in boiling salted water until tender; drain.
2. Saute onions in butter until tender but not brown.
3. Combine beaten eggs, cream, seasonings and sauteed onions. Add to noodles; toss gently.
4. Divide noodle mixture equally into unbaked pie shells. Sprinkle with grated cheese.
5. Bake in a 400°F. oven 40 to 45 minutes.
6. Let stand at least 10 minutes. Cut and serve with Savory Salmon Sauce.*

*SAVORY SALMON SAUCE

Yield: 24 portions - 3 quarts

Ingredients

SALMON, poached or steamed	4 pounds
WHITE SAUCE (made with fish liquid, if desired)	2 quarts
SALT	1½ teaspoons
PEPPER	¼ teaspoon
MUSTARD, dry	1 tablespoon
PAPRIKA	¼ teaspoon
LEMON JUICE	½ cup
WORCESTERSHIRE SAUCE	1 tablespoon
PARSLEY, chopped	1 cup

Procedure

1. Break salmon into bite-size pieces.
2. Combine white sauce with remaining ingredients. Fold in salmon
3. Heat thoroughly. Serve over wedges of noodle quiche.

DEVILED HAM AND RICE

Match with these menu mates: buttered Italian green beans, fresh spinach and mandarin orange salad and caramel custard.

Yield: 24 portions

Ingredients

DEVILED HAM	5 4½-ounce cans
MUSTARD, prepared	2 tablespoons
MAYONNAISE	2/3 cup
GREEN ONIONS, chopped	1¼ cups
CELERY SALT	1½ tablespoons
RICE, cooked	1 gallon
BACON, fried crisp, crumbled	1 pound

Procedure

1. Blend deviled ham, mustard, mayonnaise, onions and salt.
2. Toss with rice and crumbled bacon. Heat thoroughly.

BEEFY MACARONI CASSEROLE

A Bibb lettuce and mushroom salad and hot garlic buttered bread give an element of style to this homey dish. Peach halves topped with pistachio ice cream makes a pleasing dessert.

Yield: 33 8-ounce portions

Ingredients

MACARONI, elbow, uncooked	2 pounds
BEEF, ground, lean	5½ pounds
ONIONS, finely chopped	2 pounds
TOMATO SOUP, condensed	2 51-ounce cans
VINEGAR, cider	¼ cup
WORCESTERSHIRE SAUCE	2 tablespoons
SALT	1 tablespoon
PEPPER, white	½ to 1 teaspoon
CHEESE, PARMESAN	¾ cup

Procedure

1. Cook macaroni according to package directions. Drain.
2. Brown beef slowly in heavy skillet. Add onions; cook until tender.
3. Blend in soup, vinegar, seasonings and cooked macaroni.
4. Pour 2¾ quarts into each of 3 pans 12-inch by 10-inch by 2½-inch. Sprinkle with cheese.
5. Bake in a 350°F. oven 45 minutes or until lightly browned.

STUFFED MANICOTTI, HUNTER STYLE
A popular combination with a romaine salad, Italian bread and spumoni.

Yield: 24 portions (2 each)

Ingredients

CELERY, chopped	1 quart
ONION, finely chopped	2 cups
COOKING OIL	½ cup
PARSLEY, finely chopped	¼ cup
GARLIC, mashed	2 cloves
TOMATO PASTE or PUREE	1½ quarts
WATER	3 quarts
SALT	2 tablespoons
PEPPER	1 teaspoon
BASIL, dried	2 teaspoons
OREGANO, dried	1 teaspoon
BAY LEAVES	2
CHEESE, ricotta or cottage	4 pounds (2 quarts)
SPINACH, frozen, thawed, drained, chopped	3 pounds (2 quarts)
CHEESE, PARMESAN, grated	2 cups
BREAD CRUMBS, dry	1 cup
EGGS, slightly beaten	4
SALT	1 tablespoon
PEPPER	½ teaspoon
MANICOTTI, cooked	48
RIPE OLIVES, pitted, drained	1 quart
CHEESE, PARMESAN, grated	1 cup

Procedure

1. Saute celery and onion in oil until transparent. Add parsley, garlic, tomato paste, water, salt, pepper and herbs. Cover; simmer 30 to 40 minutes.

2. Drain ricotta; combine with spinach, first amount of Parmesan cheese, bread crumbs, eggs, salt and pepper.

3. Holding manicotti almost vertically, stuff each with 3 ounces spinach mixture, using pastry bag and No. 7 plain tip. Arrange 8 across and 3 down in each of 2 greased 12-inch by 20-inch by 2-inch pans.

4. Chop olives coarsely; add to sauce; bring to simmer. Remove bay leaves. Pour over manicotti allowing about 2½ quarts per pan.

5. Bake in a 375°F. oven about 20 to 30 minutes. Sprinkle with remaining Parmesan cheese; bake 10 minutes longer.

6. Let stand about 10 minutes for easier serving.

Variation

For meat sauce, brown 2 pounds ground beef in oil; combine with sauteed celery and onion in Step 1. Proceed as above.

Rice Pancakes

American Dairy Association

RICE PANCAKES

For a full-fledged menu, list with a cup of vegetable soup, grilled bacon slices and (for dessert lovers) sherbet or ice cream.

Yield: 20 portions - 40 pancakes

Ingredients

FLOUR, all-purpose	4 cups (1 pound)
BAKING POWDER	3 tablespoons
SALT	2 teaspoons
EGGS, beaten	4
MILK	3 cups
BUTTER, melted	4 ounces
HONEY	¼ cup
RICE, cooked	1½ quarts
STRAWBERRIES, sliced, sweetened	1¾ quarts

Procedure

1. Sift flour, baking powder and salt together.
2. Combine eggs, milk, butter and honey. Add to flour mixture all at once; stir only until flour is moistened (batter should be lumpy). Stir in rice.
3. Bake on hot griddle using scant ¼ cup batter per pancake.
4. Serve hot with sweetened sliced strawberries.

BAKED CHICKEN AND NOODLES

Feature with buttered green peas seasoned with celery seeds and dill, tomato slices on cress, and chocolate ice cream with chocolate sauce and pretzels.

Yield: 24 5-ounce portions

Ingredients

NOODLES, medium	12 ounces
CELERY, sliced diagonally	2 cups
ONION, chopped	½ cup
BUTTER or MARGARINE	2 ounces
CREAM OF CHICKEN SOUP, condensed	1 50-ounce can
MILK	2 cups
PIMIENTO, diced	¼ cup
CHICKEN OR TURKEY MEAT, boned, diced	2 pounds
BREAD CRUMBS, buttered	½ cup

Procedure

1. Cook noodles in unsalted water until done but firm. Drain.
2. Saute celery and onion in butter until transparent.
3. Blend soup and milk, add sauteed vegetables, pimiento and chicken; fold in noodles.
4. Pour into 12-inch by 20-inch by 2-inch baking pan. Sprinkle with buttered crumbs.
5. Bake in a 350°F. oven 45 minutes or until sauce is bubbling and crumbs are brown.

CHICKEN RISOTTO

French fried onion rings and thick slices of red ripe tomatoes make good companions for this dish.

Yield: 50 portions

Ingredients

RICE, long grain	4 pounds
BUTTER or MARGARINE	1 pound
ONIONS, chopped	1 pound
MUSHROOMS, canned, sliced	2 cups
CHICKEN MEAT, cooked, cut	6½ pounds
CHICKEN SOUP BASE	1 cup
WATER, hot	1½ gallons
PEAS, cooked	1 pound
PARMESAN CHEESE, grated	8 ounces

BAKED MACARONI AND OLIVES AU GRATIN

This dish combines successfully with a vegetable juice cocktail, apple-celery-and-nut salad and an ice cream pie.

Yield: 50 10-ounce portions

Ingredients

ELBOW MACARONI	4 pounds
BUTTER or MARGARINE	8 ounces
FLOUR	9 ounces
MILK, scalded	1¼ gallons
SALT	3 tablespoons
PEPPER	1 tablespoon
CHEESE, AMERICAN, shredded or ground	4 pounds
STUFFED GREEN OLIVES, chopped	3 cups
BREAD CRUMBS, dry	1 quart
BUTTER or MARGARINE, melted	8 ounces

Procedure

1. Cook macaroni until tender; drain well.
2. Melt butter, blend in flour. Stir in hot milk gradually. Add seasonings. Cook and stir until sauce is thickened and smooth.
3. Add cheese gradually; stir until melted. Fold in chopped olives.
4. Combine macaroni and sauce; mix well. Place in well greased baking pans.
5. Combine crumbs and melted butter; sprinkle over top of macaroni mixture.
6. Bake in a 350°F. oven until thoroughly hot and top is browned.

Procedure

1. Lightly brown rice in butter. Add onions and mushrooms; saute until golden, not brown.
2. Divide evenly in two 12-inch by 20-inch by 4-inch pans.
3. Divide chicken evenly between the two pans.
4. Mix soup base and water. Pour half into each pan; mix thoroughly.
5. Cover pans. Bake in a 425°F. oven 20 minutes. Mix lightly with fork.
6. Add peas; bake 5 more minutes.
7. Sprinkle with cheese. Bake, uncovered, 5 more minutes.

TUNA CASSEROLE SUPREME

A tuna and noodle dish with a new dimension. Serve with a tossed green salad sprinkled with croutons and add a pear and gingerbread upside-down cake for dessert.

Yield: 24 portions

Ingredients

WIDE NOODLES	1 pound
TUNA	4 13-ounce cans
TOMATO SAUCE	3½ cups
COTTAGE CHEESE, small curd	2 pounds
SOUR CREAM	2 cups
GREEN ONIONS, chopped	1 cup
RIPE OLIVES, chopped	½ cup
GREEN PEPPER, chopped	¼ cup
SALT	2 teaspoons

Procedure

1. Cook noodles according to package directions; drain.
2. Break tuna into bite-size pieces; combine with tomato sauce.
3. Combine cottage cheese, sour cream, onions, olives, green pepper and salt; mix well.
4. Spread half of the noodles in a well greased 12-inch by 20-inch by 2-inch pan; top with tuna mixture. Cover with remaining noodles. Spread with cottage cheese mixture.
5. Cover pan with foil. Bake in a 350°F. oven 35 to 40 minutes. Allow to stand about 10 minutes before serving.

TOMATO RICE AU GRATIN

To round out the menu, add green beans with almonds, skewered fruits (prunes, pineapple chunks and whole strawberries) on romaine and English trifle.

Yield: 50 portions

Ingredients

RICE, uncooked	4 pounds
ONIONS, chopped	1 pound
BUTTER or SHORTENING	4 ounces
CHICKEN SOUP BASE	1 cup
WATER	1 gallon
TOMATOES, canned with juice	1½ gallons
CHEDDAR CHEESE, grated	6¼ pounds

BEEF RICE CASSEROLE

With this, serve green and wax beans, lettuce hearts with blue cheese dressing and red cherry tarts.

Yield: 48 portions

Ingredients

RICE	2 pounds
CELERY, finely diced	2 pounds
ONIONS, finely chopped	8 ounces
SHORTENING	½ cup
CREAM OF TOMATO SOUP	3 51-ounce cans
WATER	1 quart
GROUND BEEF	6 pounds
SHORTENING	½ cup
SALT	2 tablespoons
PEPPER	1 teaspoon

Procedure

1. Cook rice; drain. Turn into two 18-inch by 12-inch by 2-inch pans.

2. Saute celery and onions in first amount of shortening until lightly browned. Spoon over rice.

3. Combine soup with water. Pour 1 quart into each pan.

4. Brown beef in remaining shortening. Add salt and pepper. Spoon into pans, dividing mixture equally between the two pans.

5. Pour remaining soup mixture over meat. Using a fork, make tunnels in mixture to allow soup to seep to bottom.

6. Bake in a 375°F. oven 1 hour or until thoroughly hot and lightly browned.

▼ ▼

Procedure

1. Divide rice between two 12-inch by 20-inch by 2-inch baking pans.

2. Saute onions in butter until just tender. Add soup base, water and tomatoes; bring to a boil.

3. Pour over rice in each pan; mix well. Cover pans; bake in a 400°F. oven 25 minutes or until rice is tender.

4. Stir 2 pounds of cheese into each pan; sprinkle tops with remaining cheese. Return to oven for 5 minutes to melt cheese.

BAKED TUNA AND NOODLES AU GRATIN

Serve with a tossed salad of greens and orange sections, crisp-crusted hard rolls and angel food cake with strawberry ice cream.

Yield: 25 portions

Ingredients

NOODLES, medium	12 ounces
ONIONS, chopped	2 cups
SHORTENING	2 tablespoons
CREAM OF CELERY SOUP, condensed	1 50 or 51-ounce can
MILK	1½ cups
TUNA, drained, flaked	3 13-ounce cans
CHEESE, sharp, shredded	1 pound (1 quart)
FROZEN PEAS, cooked	2 cups
BREAD CRUMBS, buttered	1 cup
PAPRIKA	as needed

Procedure

1. Cook noodles in unsalted water; rinse and drain.
2. Cook onion in shortening until tender; add soup and milk; stir until smooth.
3. Fold in cooked noodles, tuna, 2 cups shredded cheese and peas.
4. Turn into a 12-inch by 18-inch by 2-inch baking pan. Top with remaining cheese; sprinkle with crumbs; sprinkle with paprika.
5. Bake in a 400ºF. oven 30 to 40 minutes or until sauce is bubbling and crumbs are brown.

NOODLE AND APPLESAUCE BAKE

Serve with slices of cold corned beef and round out the menu with a jellied beet and horseradish salad and chocolate cup cakes.

Yield: 48 portions

Ingredients

BROAD NOODLES	3 pounds
BUTTER or MARGARINE, melted	12 ounces
EGGS, beaten	12
APPLESAUCE	1 No. 10 can
SALT	1 tablespoon
CLOVES, ground	2 teaspoons
SUGAR, brown	9 ounces
CHEESE, AMERICAN, grated	1½ pounds
BREAD CRUMBS, dry	1 quart
BUTTER or MARGARINE, melted	4 ounces

SALMON-NOODLE BAKE

Try as a menu combination with green peas and celery, a grapefruit salad and chocolate walnut drop cookies.

Yield: 24 portions

Ingredients

EGG NOODLES, medium	10 ounces
CELERY, ¼-inch dice	2 cups
ONION, chopped	1 cup
BUTTER or MARGARINE	2 to 3 tablespoons
CREAM OF MUSHROOM SOUP	1 50-ounce can
MILK	2 cups
RIPE OLIVES, sliced	1 cup
GREEN PEPPER, diced	½ cup
CHEESE, CHEDDAR, shredded	1 pound
SALMON (canned), drained, flaked	2 pounds
BREAD CRUMBS, fine dry	as needed
PAPRIKA	as needed

Procedure

1. Cook noodles according to package directions.
2. Saute celery and onion in butter until onion is transparent.
3. Blend in soup, milk, olives, green pepper and half of the cheese. Fold in salmon and noodles.
4. Turn into greased steam table pan 12-inch by 18-inch by 2-inch. Sprinkle top with remaining cheese, bread crumbs and paprika.
5. Bake in a 350°F. oven for 45 minutes or until mixture is hot and bubbly.

▼   ▼

Procedure

1. Cook noodles; drain. While hot, combine with first amount of butter and eggs.
2. Divide half of the noodle mixture evenly into two greased 12-inch by 20-inch by 2-inch baking pans.
3. Combine applesauce, salt, cloves and brown sugar. Spread half of the mixture over noodles. Top with half of the cheese.
4. Repeat layers, using remainder of noodles and applesauce.
5. Combine remaining cheese with crumbs; toss with remaining butter. Sprinkle over each pan.
6. Bake in a 350°F. oven 45 minutes. Serve hot.

TUNA TETRAZZINI

Accompany with a tossed salad garnished with tomato wedges; add a portion of lemon sherbet sauced with dark sweet cherries.

Yield: 50 portions–Approx. ¾ cup tuna misture, ½ cup spaghetti

Ingredients

SPAGHETTI	3¼ pounds
TUNA, canned, separated into bite-size pieces	5 quarts
ONIONS, chopped	2 cups
PARSLEY, chopped	½ cup
MUSHROOMS, sliced	3 8-ounce cans
PIMIENTOS, cut in strips	2 cups
BECHAMEL SAUCE	1½ gallons
SHERRY WINE	1 cup
SALT	as needed
PEPPER	as needed
CHEESE, SWISS, grated	½ pound

Procedure

1. Cook spaghetti in boiling salted water until tender. Drain; rinse in hot water.

2. Mix tuna with onions, parsley, mushrooms, pimientos, Bechamel sauce and sherry. Season with salt and pepper.

3. Grease individual casseroles or baking pans. Cover bottoms with hot spaghetti. Ladle hot tuna mixture on top. Sprinkle with grated cheese (more, or less as desired).

4. Place under broiler or in hot oven until brown and bubbly. Garnish with a sprig of parsley.

Tuna Tetrazzini

National Canners Association

FISH TETRAZZINI

Try featuring with a cranberry juice cocktail, Italian bread sticks and a fresh fruit cup.

Yield: 16 portions

Ingredients

SPAGHETTI	1 pound
ONION, chopped	2/3 cup
BUTTER or MARGARINE	2 ounces
CREAM OF MUSHROOM SOUP, condensed	1 50-ounce can
WATER	1-1/2 cups
CHEESE, ROMANO, grated	1 cup
FISH, flaked*	2 pounds
RIPE OLIVES, pitted, chopped	1-1/3 cups
PARSLEY, chopped	1/4 cup
LEMON JUICE	1-1/2 tablespoons
THYME	1/8 teaspoon
MARJORAM	1/8 teaspoon

Procedure

1. Cook spaghetti until tender; drain.
2. Saute onions in butter until golden.
3. Combine onions with soup, water and ½ of the cheese. Mix well. Fold in fish and remaining ingredients; heat thoroughly.
4. Gently mix sauce with spaghetti. Place in well greased individual casseroles; sprinkle with remaining cheese.
5. Bake in a 350°F. oven 25 to 30 minutes.

*May substitute shrimp and/or clams, if desired.

SHRIMP PILAF

Present this well-seasoned dish with a green salad tossed with pieces of avocado and slices of egg. And, for dessert, offer apricot halves topped with orange sherbet and a splash of Cointreau.

Yield: 50 portions

Ingredients

RICE, uncooked	2 quarts
BUTTER or MARGARINE	12 ounces
ONIONS, chopped	8 medium
GREEN PEPPERS, diced	1½ quarts
CELERY, diced	2½ quarts
TOMATO JUICE	1½ gallons
BEEF BOUILLON	2½ quarts
PARSLEY, minced	1½ cups
CAYENNE	2 teaspoons
SUMMER SAVORY	2 teaspoons
SALT	4 teaspoons
SHRIMP, cooked, peeled, deveined	8 pounds
GUMBO FILE	1 teaspoon

Procedure

1. Saute rice in butter, stirring frequently, until golden brown.

2. Stir in onions, peppers, celery, tomato juice and bouillon. Cover tightly; bake in a 375°F. oven 30 minutes.

3. Stir lightly with fork. Add parsley, cayenne, summer savory, salt and shrimp.

4. Return to oven; cook 20 minutes. Stir in gumbo file.

CLAM PANTRY PASTA

Shell macaroni, green noodles and minced clams join forces to create a distinctive pasta dish to feature on the menu with broiled tomato halves, crisp celery hearts and for dessert, coconut topped orange slices with bite-size brownies.

Yield: 24 portions

Ingredients

MACARONI, shell or elbow	1½ quarts
GREEN NOODLES	1½ quarts
CLAMS, minced (canned)	3 quarts
ONION FLAKES	½ cup
CLAM LIQUID	½ cup
BUTTER or MARGARINE	6 ounces
FLOUR	1/3 cup
INSTANT GARLIC POWDER	¼ teaspoon
BLACK PEPPER, ground	½ teaspoon
MILK	1½ cups
CLAM LIQUID	1 quart
PARSLEY FLAKES	¾ cup
CHEESE, creamed cottage or ricotta	1½ quarts
CHEESE, PARMESAN, grated	¾ cup

Procedure

1. Cook macaroni and noodles separately until tender. Rinse; drain well.

2. Drain minced clams; reserve liquid.

3. Combine onion flakes with first amount of clam liquid; let stand 10 minutes to soften.

4. Saute softened onion in butter until golden. Blend in flour, garlic powder and pepper. Add milk and remaining clam liquid. Cook and stir over low heat until smooth and slightly thickened. Stir in parsley flakes.

5. Layer about half the cooked macaroni and the cooked noodles in a buttered 12-inch by 20-inch by 2-inch baking pan.

6. Cover with cottage or ricotta cheese and clams. Top with remaining pasta. Pour clam sauce over all. Sprinkle with Parmesan cheese.

7. Cover; bake in a 350°F. oven 30 to 40 minutes or until heated throughout.

FISH, NOODLES AND MUSHROOMS

Offer with buttered chopped broccoli and a sliced cucumber salad with lemon chiffon pie on the program for dessert.

Yield: 50 6-ounce portions

Ingredients

NOODLES	1½ pounds
ONIONS, chopped	1½ cups
BUTTER or MARGARINE	1 pound
FLOUR	¾ cup
SALT	as needed
PEPPER	½ teaspoon
MILK	3 quarts
WORCESTERSHIRE SAUCE	2½ teaspoons
PIMIENTOS, chopped	1 cup
MUSHROOMS, stems and pieces	8 8-ounce cans
MUSHROOM LIQUID	1 quart
BUTTER or MARGARINE	½ pound
FISH FLAKES	9 15-ounce cans
BREAD CRUMBS, soft	1 quart
BUTTER or MARGARINE, melted	as needed

Procedure

1. Cook noodles in boiling salted water. Drain.
2. Saute onion in first amount of butter until tender but not brown.
3. Blend in flour, salt and pepper. Add milk; cook and stir until thickened. Add Worcestershire sauce and pimientos.
4. Drain mushrooms, reserving required amount of liquid. Add mushroom liquid to sauce.
5. Brown mushrooms lightly in next amount of butter; add to sauce.
6. Put a layer of noodles in each of two 12-inch by 18-inch by 2-inch baking pans. Add a layer of fish. Cover with sauce; sprinkle top with bread crumbs
7. Drizzle a little melted butter over bread crumbs. Bake in a 350°F. oven about 40 minutes, until heated through and crumbs brown.

Variations

For salmon, noodles and mushrooms, use 9 1-pound cans salmon, flaked, in place of fish flakes. For Tuna, Noodles and Mushrooms, use 11 13-ounce cans tuna, flaked, in place of fish flakes.

EASY LASAGNE

Serve with a crisp green salad tossed with anchovy dressing. Offer coffee gelatin with custard sauce as dessert.

Yield: 48 portions

Ingredients

GROUND BEEF	3 pounds
COOKING OIL	as needed
INSTANT CHOPPED ONION	½ cup
INSTANT GRANULATED GARLIC	¾ teaspoon
TOMATOES, canned	4 pounds
TOMATO PASTE	2 cups
OREGANO	1 tablespoon
PARSLEY, chopped	3 tablespoons
PEPPER	½ teaspoon
WATER	3 cups
LASAGNE NOODLES	1½ pounds
CHEESE, MOZZARELLA, sliced	2¼ pounds
CHEESE, process American, sliced	1½ pounds
CHEESE, Parmesan, shredded	1½ cups

Procedure

1. Brown ground beef in a small amount of oil. Add onion, garlic, tomatoes, tomato paste, oregano, parsley, pepper and water. Simmer ½ hour.

2. Cook noodles in large amount of boiling salted water until tender. Drain.

3. Place half the noodles in two 12-inch by 20-inch steam table pans. Top with half of the meat sauce and Mozzarella. Repeat these layers.

4. Top with American and Parmesan cheeses.

5. Bake in a 350°F. oven 30 to 35 minutes. Let stand 15 minutes for easier cutting and serving.

American Dairy Association

TURKEY AND HAM TETRAZZINI

Combine with a leafy green salad and a Napoleon slice.

Yield: 48 portions

Ingredients

SPAGHETTI	3¼ pounds
ONIONS, chopped	2 cups
CELERY, chopped	2 cups
BUTTER or MARGARINE	4 ounces
MUSHROOMS, sliced, drained	3 8-ounce cans
WHITE SAUCE, medium, well seasoned	1½ gallons
SHERRY	1 cup
TURKEY ROLL, diced	3 quarts
HAM, canned, diced	2 quarts
PIMIENTOS, cut in strips	2 cups
PARSLEY, chopped	¾ cup
SALT	as needed
PEPPER	as needed
CHEESE, SWISS, grated	½ to ¾ pound

Procedure

1. Cook spaghetti until just tender; drain; rinse.

2. Saute onions and celery in butter until softened but not brown. Add drained mushrooms.

3. Combine white sauce and sherry; add vegetable mixture, diced turkey roll, ham, pimiento and parsley. Season with salt and pepper.

4. Put spaghetti in two greased 12-inch by 20-inch by 2-inch pans. Ladle hot turkey and ham mixture over top.

5. Sprinkle with cheese. Place under broiler or in a 400°F. oven until brown and bubbly.

CHIPPED BEEF AND NOODLE CASSEROLE

Present with spiced peach halves and green bean succotash. Offer raspberry sherbet and a frosted cake square for dessert.

Yield: 48 portions

Ingredients

NOODLES	2¼ pounds
BUTTER or MARGARINE	½ pound
FLOUR	6 ounces
MILK	3 quarts
PEPPER, white	2 teaspoons
CHEESE, CHEDDAR, shredded	2 pounds
MUSHROOMS, fresh, sliced	2 pounds
BUTTER or MARGARINE	2 ounces
CHIPPED BEEF	2¼ pounds
BACON FAT	1 cup
PIMIENTOS, diced	1 cup
BREAD CRUMBS, soft	1 quart
BUTTER or MARGARINE, melted	¼ pound

Procedure

1. Cook noodles until tender; drain.
2. Melt first amount of butter; blend in flour. Add milk gradually; cook and stir until sauce is thickened and smooth. Add pepper.
3. Remove sauce from heat. Add cheese; stir until blended.
4. Saute mushrooms in next amount of butter until tender. Add to cheese sauce.
5. Saute chipped beef in bacon fat until edges curl.
6. Combine noodles, cheese sauce, chipped beef and pimientos. Turn into two 14-inch by 9-inch by 2-inch baking pans.
7. Toss crumbs with melted butter. Sprinkle evenly over top of pans.
8. Bake in a 375°F. oven until thoroughly hot and crumbs are brown.

LOBSTER-RICE CASSEROLE WITH SHERRY SAUCE
Try featuring with a mimosa salad and a strawberry parfait.

Yield: 48 portions

Ingredients

ONION, finely chopped	1½ cups
BUTTER or MARGARINE	1½ pounds
FLOUR	10 ounces
NONFAT DRY MILK	1½ pounds
WATER, warm	1½ gallons
SALT	2 tablespoons
PEPPER, white	1 teaspoon
LIQUID HOT PEPPER SEASONING	few drops
NUTMEG	¼ teaspoon
SHERRY	1½ to 2 cups
RICE, cooked, hot	1½ gallons
LOBSTER MEAT	6 pounds
PAPRIKA	as needed

Procedure

1. Saute onion in butter until tender, but not brown. Remove from heat.

2. Sift flour and non-fat dry milk together. Blend with butter and onion.

3. Add warm water, stirring until smooth. Bring sauce slowly to a boil, stirring.

4. Remove from heat; add seasonings. Keep hot over hot water. Add sherry just before using.

5. To serve, place ½ cup rice in casserole. Top with 2 ounces lobster. Pour 5 ounces sauce over lobster. Sprinkle with paprika. Run under broiler until bubbly and lightly browned.

American Dairy Association

FIESTA RICE 'N CHEESE

Try completing the menu with buttered green peas and sliced water chestnuts, hearts of romaine with Chiffonade dressing and warm peach halves a la mode.

Yield: 96 portions

Ingredients

RICE, long grained, uncooked	5 pounds
CELERY, thinly sliced	2 pounds
GREEN PEPPER, chopped	2 pounds
ONION, chopped	1¼ pounds
BUTTER or MARGARINE	1 pound
CREAM OF MUSHROOM SOUP, condensed	4 50-ounce cans
MUSTARD, prepared	½ cup
MARJORAM, leaf, crushed	1/4 to 1/3 cup
CHEESE, sharp cheddar, shredded	12 pounds
TOMATO, fresh, ½-inch pieces	8 pounds
BREAD CRUMBS, buttered	1 quart
GREEN PEPPER RINGS (thin)	96

Procedure

1. Cook rice according to package directions.

2. Saute celery, chopped green pepper and onion in butter until celery is tender crisp and starts to look transparent.

3. Combine soup, mustard and marjoram; mix well. Fold in cooked rice, sauteed vegetables, cheese and tomatoes.

4. Put into 4 greased 12-inch by 20-inch by 2½-inch pans, allowing 1 gallon, 2½ quarts per pan.

5. Top with buttered crumbs.

6. Bake in a 350°F. oven 45 to 60 minutes or until hot and bubbly.

7. Remove from oven. Arrange green pepper rings on top to indicate portions.

RICE CROQUETTES WITH HOT SPICED APPLESAUCE

These croquettes make a fine alliance with grilled small ham steaks.

Yield: 50 portions

Ingredients

RICE	2½ pounds
SALT	3 tablespoons
CAYENNE PEPPER	¼ to ½ teaspoon
APPLE JUICE	3 quarts
CHEESE, CHEDDAR, diced	3 pounds
EGGS, beaten	2 pounds
CRACKER CRUMBS	2 cups
ONION JUICE	¼ cup
WORCESTERSHIRE SAUCE	3 tablespoons
PARSLEY, chopped	3 cups
CEREAL FLAKES*	6 quarts
APPLESAUCE	1½ No. 10 cans
CINNAMON	4 teaspoons

Procedure

1. Cook rice with salt and cayenne in apple juice until rice is tender and juice has been absorbed. Remove from heat.
2. Combine rice with cheese, eggs, cracker crumbs, onion juice, Worcestershire and parsley.
3. Cool thoroughly.
4. Crush cereal flakes lightly.
5. Shape rice mixture into 100 croquettes using No. 24 scoop.
6. Roll in cereal; place on greased baking sheet.
7. Bake in a 425°F. oven 10 minutes.
8. Combine applesauce and cinnamon. Heat. Serve hot over rice croquettes, allowing 2 ounces per portion.

*Or cornflake crumbs, 1½ pounds.

Mushroom Beef Burgers (see recipe, p. 102)

SANDWICHES

SANDWICH meals get a popular vote. What's more, they are easy to prepare and serve. Encourage the trend and offer a sandwich menu that's alive and inviting. Try new ideas in fillings, pleasing change-abouts in bread.

With cold sandwiches and hot, open-face and closed, there's simply no end to the taste-tempting variety that you can command.

As to presentation, your choice of a plate—or maybe a well-suited basket or little tray—can spell the difference. And never underestimate the effect of a ravishing garnish!

Sandwiches and soup are boon companions. But, being congenial partners, sandwiches team equally well with fruit or vegetable juices, perky salads, milk shakes and other beverages.

BACON-AVOCADO CLUB SANDWICH

Garnish with ripe olives and celery hearts and list with baked custard and coconut macaroons as dessert.

Yield: 50 sandwiches

Ingredients

AVOCADO, thinly sliced	12 (6 pounds)
LEMON JUICE	1 cup
BACON, fried crisp	100 slices (5 pounds)
TOMATOES	100 slices (6 pounds)
LETTUCE	as needed
SALAD DRESSING	as needed
ENRICHED TOAST, buttered	150 slices

Procedure

1. Sprinkle avocado with lemon juice; mix lightly.
2. Make club sandwiches using 3 slices of buttered toast. Fill first layer with avocado and 2 slices of bacon; fill second with 2 slices tomato, lettuce and salad dressing.

BARBECUED HAMBURGER SANDWICHES

Serve with a mixed fruit salad on the side.

Yield: 50 sandwiches

Ingredients

BEEF, lean, ground	7 pounds
ONION, finely cut	1½ cups
INSTANT NONFAT DRY MILK	1 quart
SALT	3 tablespoons
PEPPER	1 teaspoon
CHILI POWDER	2 tablespoons
DRY MUSTARD	1 tablespoon
TOMATO PUREE	½ No. 10 can
SANDWICH BUNS, sliced	50

Procedure

1. Brown beef and onion slowly, stirring occasionally with a fork to break up meat.
2. Mix instant dry milk, salt, pepper, chili powder and dry mustard. Add tomato puree in two additions, beating with a French whip until smooth.
3. Add sauce to meat mixture. Heat until thoroughly hot and flavors are blended.
4. To serve: Place a No. 24 scoop of mixture in each bun.

OPEN HAM SANDWICH WITH CREAMY COLE SLAW TOPPING

Combine with cream of spinach soup and fruited raspberry gelatine.

Yield: 24 sandwiches

Ingredients

CABBAGE, shredded	1 quart
CARROT, grated	2 cups
ONION, chopped	½ cup
SALAD DRESSING	1 cup
CURRY POWDER	1 teaspoon
HAM, ¼-inch slices	24
BREAD SLICES, buttered	24

Procedure

1. Combine cabbage, carrot, onion, salad dressing and curry powder. Add salt to season, if desired.

2. For each sandwich, place ham slice on a slice of buttered bread. Top with ¼ cup of cole slaw. Garnish with sliced ripe olives, if desired.

HAM SANDWICH, GERMAN STYLE

Presented with hot potato salad, this offering takes nothing more than a compote of fruit to make a pleasing meal.

Yield: 24 sandwiches

Ingredients

HAM SLICES	24
RYE BREAD, buttered	48 slices
SAUERKRAUT, drained	1½ quarts
SWISS CHEESE slices	24
SALAD DRESSING	¾ cup
CATSUP	¾ cup

Procedure

1. Place a slice of ham on the unbuttered side of each of 24 slices of bread.

2. Arrange ¼ cup drained sauerkraut on each ham slice. Cover sauerkraut with slice of Swiss cheese.

3. Combine salad dressing with catsup. Spread on unbuttered side of remaining bread. Place on cheese, buttered side up.

4. Grill slowly on both sides until sandwich is browned and cheese is melted.

5. Serve with hot potato salad, if desired.

CHEESE AND DEVILED EGG SANDWICHES

The meal is completed by a bowl of soup, hefty with vegetables and chocolate cake squares with ice cream as the dessert.

Yield: 24 Sandwiches

Ingredients

COTTAGE CHEESE, creamed	2½ pounds
EGGS, hard-cooked, finely chopped	8
SALT	2 teaspoons
DRY MUSTARD	1½ teaspoons
SOUR CREAM (commercial)	1 cup
ENRICHED WHITE BREAD, buttered	24 slices
WHOLE WHEAT BREAD, buttered	24 slices

Procedure

1. Combine cottage cheese and eggs.
2. Mix salt and mustard; add to sour cream; blend. Add to cheese mixture; mix thoroughly.
3. Make sandwiches using a No. 20 scoop of filling between one slice of white bread, one of whole wheat bread.

CHILI BURGERS

Try presenting with corn chips and tomato slices topped with chopped green onions.

Yield: 24 portions

Ingredients

SWEET PEPPER FLAKES	¼ cup
INSTANT MINCED ONION	¼ cup
WATER	½ cup
BEEF, ground	6 pounds
SALT	2 tablespoons
CHILI POWDER	2 tablespoons
INSTANT GARLIC POWDER	1 teaspoon
BLACK PEPPER, ground	1 teaspoon
HAMBURGER BUNS, warm	24

Procedure

1. Combine pepper flakes, instant minced onion and water; let stand 10 minutes.
2. Combine beef, seasonings and the hydrated vegetables. Do not overmix.
3. Shape into 4-ounce patties about 4 inches across. Broil, turning once, cooking to desired doneness. Serve on warm buns.

COMIN' THRU THE RYE

Garnish with pickles and round out the menu with chilled vegetable juice, fresh pears and chocolate chip cookies.

Yield: 48 portions

Ingredients

CABBAGE, shredded	3¾ pounds
COLESLAW DRESSING	3 cups
RYE BREAD, sliced	96 slices
CHEESE, Swiss, sliced	5 pounds
CORNED BEEF, cooked, sliced	6 pounds
SHORTENING, frying	as needed

Procedure

1. Combine cabbage and dressing; toss lightly, mixing well. Chill.
2. For each sandwich: Cover one slice of bread with 1/3 cup coleslaw, a 1½-ounce slice of Swiss cheese, 2 ounces corned beef and another slice of bread.
3. Brush both sides of sandwich with shortening; grill until cheese is melted and bread is lightly browned.

SAUERKRAUT-CHEESE TOPPED FRANKFURTER SANDWICHES

Serve with a tasty potato salad and offer chilled slices of watermelon for dessert.

Yield: 100 portions

Ingredients

SAUERKRAUT, canned, drained	1½ gallons
CHEESE, cheddar, shredded	3 pounds
BUTTER or MARGARINE	1 pound
FRANKFURTER ROLLS	100
FRANKFURTERS (8 to pound)	100

Procedure

1. Place two-thirds of the sauerkraut in a colander; rinse with boiling water. Mix with remaining third. Drain well.
2. Toss drained sauerkraut and shredded cheese together, mixing thoroughly.
3. Spread butter on each roll; place a frankfurter on the bottom half of each one. Top each frankfurter with ¼ cup of the sauerkraut mixture.
4. Place on baking sheets; bake in a 400°F. oven 10 minutes or place under broiler until cheese is bubbly. Top with other half of roll.

SWISS-TURKEY SANDWICH

Good all the way when the meal includes chicken noodle soup and glazed fruit tarts.

Yield: 24 sandwiches

Ingredients

BREAD, large rye	24 slices
BUTTER (optional)	as needed
LETTUCE	24 leaves
TURKEY ROLL, sliced	4½ pounds
CHEESE, SWISS, sliced	2¼ pounds
BACON SLICES, crisp	48 slices
THOUSAND ISLAND DRESSING	1½ quarts
TOMATO WEDGES	48

Procedure

1. Spread bread with butter, if desired. Cover with lettuce.
2. Add sliced turkey and Swiss cheese allowing 3 ounces turkey and 1½ ounces cheese per sandwich.
3. Just before serving, top each sandwich with 2 slices bacon. Cover with ¼ cup dressing. Garnish with 2 tomato wedges.

CHEESE BARBECUE SANDWICH

These tasty cheese buns contrast nicely with tomato soup. Try offering individual crushed pineapple upside-down cakes for dessert.

Yield: 25 sandwiches

Ingredients

CHEESE, AMERICAN, grated	1½ pounds
GREEN PEPPERS, chopped	½ cup
ONIONS, finely chopped	¼ cup
GREEN OLIVES, stuffed, chopped	¾ cup
EGGS, hard-cooked, chopped	8
CATSUP	¾ cup
BUTTER or MARGARINE, melted	¼ cup
SANDWICH ROLLS, sliced	25

Procedure

1. Combine cheese, green pepper, onions, olives, eggs, catsup and melted butter; mix.
2. Spread a No. 24 scoop of the mixture on bottom half of each roll.
3. Place both halves under broiler until tops of rolls toast and cheese melts. Serve immediately.

PINEAPPLE FRENCH TOAST SANDWICHES
Just add a Waldorf salad, hot cocoa and cookies.

Yield: 50 sandwiches

Ingredients

CREAM CHEESE	2 pounds
CRUSHED PINEAPPLE, drained	1 quart
SALT	1 teaspoon
RAISIN BREAD	100 slices
EGGS, slightly beaten	1 quart (2 pounds)
MILK	1 quart
SALT	1 tablespoon

Procedure

1. Combine cream cheese, pineapple and first amount of salt. Spread a No. 30 scoop of filling on half the slices of bread. Cover with remaining slices.

2. Combine eggs, milk and remaining salt.

3. Dip sandwiches in egg mixture until well coated. Cook on well-greased griddle, turning to brown both sides.

4. Serve hot with maple syrup.

OPEN CHEESE AND FRANKFURTER SANDWICHES
Potato chips and cabbage slaw complete the plate.

Yield: 24 portions

Ingredients

MUSTARD, powdered	1 tablespoon
WATER	1 tablespoon
BUTTER or MARGARINE, softened	½ pound
INSTANT GARLIC POWDER	½ teaspoon
BREAD SLICES	48
CHEESE, AMERICAN, 1-ounce slices	48
FRANKFURTERS	24
BUTTER or MARGARINE, melted	1/3 cup

Procedure

1. Mix mustard and water; let stand 10 minutes. Combine with softened butter and instant garlic powder; mix well.

2. Spread bread. Top each slice with cheese.

3. Cut frankfurters in half lengthwise; place one half across each slice of cheese-topped bread. Brush with melted butter.

4. Broil until cheese melts. Serve hot.

THE SALMONDILLY SANDWICH

Follow this robust open-face sandwich with lemon sherbet served in a parfait glass with fruit cocktail.

Yield: 25 sandwiches

Ingredients

SALMON, red	3 1-pound cans
DILL PICKLES, cross cut	1 quart
ONIONS, sliced	1 pound
BREAD, dark rye	25 slices
BUTTER or MARGARINE, softened	¼ pound
EGGS, hard-cooked, sliced	12
THOUSAND ISLAND DRESSING	2 quarts

Procedure

1. Remove skin and bones from salmon; flake fish. Drain pickles, reserving juice.

2. Pour pickle juice over onions; marinate for one hour.

3. Spread bread with butter. Arrange 3 or 4 marinated onion slices on each slice of bread.

4. Place ¼ cup flaked salmon over onions. Cover salmon with hard cooked egg slices.

5. Arrange 4 or 5 dill pickle slices on top of egg slices.

6. Ladle 2½ ounces Thousand Island Dressing over sandwich. Garnish with chopped pickles, if desired.

Salmondilly Sandwich

Pickle Packers International, Inc.

STEAK SANDWICH DIANE

Feature with green salad tossed with tomato, green pepper and sliced raw cauliflower buds.

Yield: 24

Ingredients

COOKING OIL	2 cups
DRY MUSTARD	1 ounce
SALT	2 ounces
BLACK PEPPER	½ teaspoon
BUTTER	4 ounces
WORCESTERSHIRE SAUCE	¼ cup
CHIVES, minced	2 tablespoons
LEMON JUICE	¾ cup
STEAKS, rib eye, 6-ounce*	24
TOAST	48 slices
LEMON SLICES	24

Procedure

1. Blend oil, mustard, salt and pepper.
2. Melt butter; add Worcestershire, chives and lemon juice. Keep warm.
3. Coat each steak on both sides with seasoned oil mixture.
4. Broil or pan fry steaks to order.
5. Serve steak on toast with a teaspoon of the butter sauce and a slice of lemon on top. (Stir sauce thoroughly before each serving.)

*Or, 4-ounce beef tenderloin or top Butt steaks.

POLYNESIAN HAMBURGERS

Serve with peach halves filled with chutney and offer lime chiffon pie to complete the meal.

Yield: 48 portions

Ingredients

BEEF, lean ground	12 pounds
INSTANT ONION POWDER	5 tablespoons
SALT	4 teaspoons
SOY SAUCE	1 quart
GINGER, ground	4 teaspoons
BLACK PEPPER, ground	4 teaspoons
INSTANT GARLIC POWDER	1 teaspoon
HAMBURGER BUNS	48

BAKED TURKEY AND ASPARAGUS SANDWICH AU GRATIN

Companionable menu items include jellied madrilene and strawberry ice cream with strawberry sauce.

Yield: 15 sandwiches

Ingredients

TOAST SLICES	30
TURKEY, cooked, thinly sliced	2 pounds
ASPARAGUS SPEARS, cooked	60 (about 2 pounds frozen)
CREAM OF CHICKEN SOUP, condensed	1 50-ounce can
MILK	1½ cups
WORCESTERSHIRE	1 tablespoon
CHEESE, sharp, shredded	½ pound
PIMIENTO, cut in strips	as needed

Procedure

1. In individual flat oval baking dish, arrange one slice of toast in center, with a toast triangle at each side.

2. Place 2 ounces turkey meat on each sandwich; top with 4 asparagus spears.

3. Blend soup, milk and Worcestershire.

4. Ladle 4 ounces of soup mixture over asparagus and turkey. Sprinkle with cheese, allowing about 2 tablespoons per portion. Garnish with 3 strips pimiento.

5. Bake in 450°F. oven for about 10 minutes or until sauce is bubbling and cheese is lightly browned.

▼   ▼

Procedure

1. Mix ground beef, onion powder and salt. Do not overmix.

2. Shape into 4-ounce patties. Place in baking pan.

3. Combine soy sauce, ginger, black pepper and garlic powder; mix well. Pour over hamburgers. Marinate in refrigerator 30 to 45 minutes.

4. Remove hamburgers from marinade. Broil to desired doneness. Serve on warmed hamburger buns.

TUNA-CHEESE CLUB SANDWICHES

Garnish with walnut-stuffed spiced prunes cradled in a small lettuce cup and offer whipped lime gelatin with custard sauce for dessert.

Yield: 16

Ingredients

TUNA FISH, drained	14 ounces
OLIVES, stuffed, chopped	1 cup
EGGS, hard-cooked, chopped	2
LEMON JUICE	1 tablespoon
MAYONNAISE or SALAD DRESSING	2/3 cup
WHITE BREAD, toasted	32 slices
WHOLE WHEAT BREAD, toasted	16 slices
BUTTER, softened	1/2 pound
LETTUCE LEAVES	16
CHEESE, AMERICAN, 1-ounce slices	32

Procedure

1. Combine tuna, olives, eggs, lemon juice and mayonnaise; mix well.

2. Butter toast; spread 16 white slices with tuna mixture. Top each with a lettuce leaf, then a slice of whole wheat toast.

3. Cover each with 2 slices cheese, then a slice of white toast. Cut sandwiches diagonally.

CHICKEN SANDWICH AU GRATIN

This goes well with melon, served a la mode.

Yield: 25 sandwiches

Ingredients

LEMON JUICE	¼ cup
SALT	2 teaspoons
PEPPER, white	½ teaspoon
MAYONNAISE	2 cups
CHICKEN, cooked, chopped	2 pounds
CELERY, coarsely chopped	1 pound
BREAD, toasted	25 slices
CHEESE, American, thin sliced	25 slices
TOMATOES (Cut in 6 wedges)	9
PICKLE RINGS	50
WATERCRESS	2 bunches

FRENCH TOASTED MUSHROOM SANDWICH

Excellent when paired with a tomato and cottage cheese salad, add a brandied dark cherry gelatin for dessert.

Yield: 24

Ingredients

BUTTER or MARGARINE	6 ounces
SALT	1/4 teaspoon
MUSHROOMS, fresh, chopped	1-1/4 gallons (4 pounds, as purchased)
ENRICHED BREAD SLICES	48
EGGS, whole	1-1/3 cups
MILK, skim	2-2/3 cups
SALT	2 teaspoons
PEPPER	1/4 teaspoon

Procedure

1. Melt half of the butter in each of two large aluminum or stainless steel skillets.

2. Add 1/8 teaspoon salt and 2½ quarts chopped mushrooms to each skillet; saute until done over medium heat.

3. Make sandwiches using a No. 16 scoop of mushroom filling between two bread slices.

4. Beat eggs, milk, remaining salt and pepper together.

5. Dip sandwiches in egg mixture coating both sides. Grill on a lightly greased griddle.

▼   ▼

Procedure

1. Combine lemon juice, seasonings and mayonnaise; mix thoroughly.

2. Pour dressing over chicken and celery; mix lightly.

3. Spread 2½ ounces of chicken mixture on each slice of toast.

4. Cut cheese slices across diagonally. Overlap two triangles of cheese on top of chicken.

5. Place under broiler until cheese melts and browns slightly.

6. Serve hot, garnished with 2 tomato wedges, 2 pickle rings, and a generous amount of watercress.

HAM-CHEESE SANDWICH

Offer with cream of corn soup and suggest whole peeled (canned) apricots and molasses cookies for dessert.

Yield: 1 gallon filling 48 sandwiches (No. 12 scoop)

Ingredients

HAM, cooked, ground	3 pounds
PREPARED MUSTARD	½ cup
PICKLE RELISH or PICCALILLI	2 cups
PROCESS CHEESE, grated	3 pounds
MAYONNAISE or SALAD DRESSING	1¼ cups
SANDWICH BUNS, sliced	48
BUTTER or MARGARINE, soft (optional)	1 pound

Procedure

1. Combine ham, mustard, pickle relish, cheese and mayonnaise; mix well.

2. Place both halves of buns on 18-inch by 26-inch by 1-inch bun pans with cut sides up, arranging so all tops are facing same direction.

3. Spread butter over both halves of buns, if desired.

4. Place a No. 12 scoop of filling on bottom half of each sliced bun. Turn scoop over and mash filling down with back of scoop before dipping up another scoopful for next bun.

5. Heat a pan of rolls at a time, as needed, in a 350°F. oven for 8 minutes or until bun top toasts and cheese melts.

Note: To substitute sliced process cheese for grated cheese, use a No. 20 scoop of ham mixture on bun half; top with a 1-ounce slice of cheese.

GRILLED HAM 'N CHEESE SANDWICHES ════════

This offering is excellent with a 3-bean salad; list a pastry-topped apricot cobbler for dessert.

Yield: 12 sandwiches

Ingredients

HAM, cooked*	12 slices
BREAD, white	24 slices
CHEESE, process American, shredded	12 ounces
OLIVES, stuffed, sliced	1½ cups
SALT	1½ teaspoons
MUSTARD, prepared	4 teaspoons
BUTTER, melted	½ pound

HAM AND EGG WICHES

Try featuring with marinated tomato and cucumber slices and lattice rhubarb pie.

Yield: 48

Ingredients

DEVILED HAM	3¼ pounds
CELERY, finely chopped	12 ounces
DILL PICKLE RELISH	3 cups
MAYONNAISE or SALAD DRESSING	¾ cup
EGGS, hard-cooked, chopped	36
STUFFED OLIVES, chopped	2 cups
ONION, finely chopped	1 cup
MAYONNAISE or SALAD DRESSING	¾ cup
PARSLEY, chopped	½ cup
PREPARED MUSTARD	½ cup
WHOLE WHEAT BREAD, slices	96
LETTUCE	as needed

Procedure

1. Combine ham, celery, relish and first amount of mayonnaise.
2. Combine eggs, olives, onions, remaining mayonnaise, parsley and mustard.
3. Spread half of the bread slices with ham mixture.
4. Spread egg salad mixture over ham mixture.
5. Top egg salad mixture with lettuce. Place remaining bread slices on top.

Procedure

1. Place ham on half the bread slices.
2. Combine cheese, olives, salt and mustard. Spread on ham slices. Top with remaining bread.
3. Brush each sandwich with melted butter. Grill on both sides until golden brown.
4. Cut each sandwich in half diagonally. Serve hot.

*Vary with turkey or canned luncheon meat, if desired.

MUSTARD HAM SANDWICH FILLING

Garnishes of ripe olives, cheese and potato chips bolster the satiety value of this item. For heartier appetites, team with tomato bouillon and blueberry-cherry pie.

Yield: 3 cups (spreads 24 sandwiches)

Ingredients

HAM, cooked, ground	8 ounces (2 cups)
MAYONNAISE	½ cup
MUSTARD, prepared	¼ cup
RIPE OLIVES, chopped	1 cup
INSTANT MINCED ONION	1 tablespoon
LEMON JUICE	1 tablespoon
CELERY, chopped	1 cup
PEPPER	1/8 teaspoon
HOT PEPPER SAUCE	2 dashes

Procedure

1. Combine all ingredients, mixing well. Refrigerate 1 hour before using.

2. Spread on square slices of buttered seeded rye bread. Top with crisp lettuce leaves and cover to make closed sandwiches.

3. Garnish each sandwich with a slice of tomato, a slice of cheese twisted on a skewer and two ripe olives. Accompany with potato chips.

Mustard-Ham Sandwich Filling

Olive Administration Committee

BAKED TUNA AND CHEESE SANDWICH

Add a side dish of red and green cabbage slaw or whole cranberry sauce.

Yield: 50 portions

Ingredients

BREAD, white	100 slices
CHEESE, CHEDDAR, grated	2 pounds
TUNA, flaked	2 pounds
ONION, finely chopped	½ cup
EGGS, well beaten	3½ pounds
SALT	2 tablespoons
MUSTARD, prepared	1 tablespoon
MILK	5 quarts

Procedure

1. Arrange 50 slices of the bread in well buttered baking pans.
2. Combine cheese, tuna and onion; mix lightly.
3. Cover bread with tuna mixture. Cover with remaining bread slices. making sandwiches.
4. Combine eggs with salt and mustard; add milk. Pour over sandwiches. Refrigerate for 1 hour.
5. Set pans in a larger pan of hot water. Bake in a 325°F. oven for 50 minutes or until custard is set and sandwiches are puffed and brown.

OLIVE CHEESE BURGERS

For added elegance, accompany with marinated artichoke hearts and pimiento strips.

Yield: 24 portions

Ingredients

BEEF, lean, ground	6 pounds
RIPE OLIVES, chopped	1½ cups
SALT	2 tablespoons
OLIVE CHEESE TOPPING*(facing page)	1 pound
HAMBURGER BUNS, split, toasted	24

Procedure

1. Mix beef, ripe olives and salt. shape into 24 patties ½-inch larger than buns. Grill or broil.
2. Top each patty with a No. 40 scoop olive cheese topping. Continue broiling just until cheese melts. (When grilling, add topping after meat is turned to allow cheese to melt as second side grills).
3. Serve on toasted buns.

BARBECUED TUNA BUNS

Good with cream of celery soup and fresh fruit cup and cookies for dessert.

Yield: 50 sandwiches No. 12 scoop

Ingredients

BUTTER or MARGARINE	½ cup
GARLIC, finely minced	1 tablespoon
CATSUP	1½ quarts
WATER	1½ cups
STUFFED OLIVES, chopped	1½ cups
LEMON JUICE	2/3 cup
WORCESTERSHIRE SAUCE	2 tablespoons
DRY MUSTARD	1 tablespoon
TUNA, drained, flaked	2¼ quarts
SANDWICH BUNS, sliced	50

Procedure

1. Melt butter in a skillet. Add garlic; saute until brown.
2. Add catsup, water, olives, lemon juice, Worcestershire sauce and mustard; simmer 10 minutes.
3. Add tuna; simmer another 5 minutes until flavors are well blended.
4. Toast buns.
5. To serve: Place a No. 12 scoop of mixture in each bun.

▼   ▼

*OLIVE CHEESE TOPPING

Yield. 24 portions

Ingredients

CHEDDAR CHEESE, grated	12 ounces
MILK	1/3 cup
RIPE OLIVES, chopped	1/2 cup

Procedure

Combine ingredients; mix thoroughly.

6 LEAGUE FISHWICH

Feature with melon balls as a starter, lemon chiffon pie for dessert.

Yield: 42 portions

Ingredients

ONION, grated	1 tablespoon
MUSTARD, prepared	2 teaspoons
SWEET PICKLE RELISH	1½ cups
TOMATO SOUP, condensed	1 51-ounce can
LEMON JUICE	½ cup
EGGS, hard-cooked, finely chopped	10 (1 quart)
FISH STICKS, frozen	6 pounds
BUTTER or MARGARINE	as needed
BREAD, white	42 slices
CHEESE, American	42 slices
BACON, crisp cooked	42 slices
EGGS, hard-cooked, sliced	as needed
OLIVES, ripe	42

Procedure

1. Combine onion, mustard and relish.

2. Using a wire whip, blend in soup. Add lemon juice gradually, beating with whip. Blend in eggs.

3. Heat mixture to a simmer. Do not boil.

4. Prepare fish sticks according to package directions.

5. Brush baking sheet with butter. Arrange bread slices on buttered sheet; top each with 3 fish sticks and a slice of cheese.

6. Bake in a 375°F. oven 5 to 10 minutes or until cheese melts.

7. To serve: place sandwich on hot plate; top with 3 ounces hot sauce. Garnish with a slice of bacon or bacon curl, a slice or two of egg and a ripe olive.

Note: For individual service, prepare with toast; place under broiler to melt cheese.

PINEAPPLE SHRIMP LUAU SANDWICH

As a menu feature, offer with a chilled avocado soup and tapioca cream pudding with a fresh coconut topping.

Yield: 29 sandwiches

Ingredients

SLICED PINEAPPLE (29 count)	1 No. 10 can
PINEAPPLE SYRUP	2 cups
LEMON JUICE	1 cup
SALAD OIL	1 cup
SEASONED SALT	2 tablespoons
SUGAR	4 teaspoons
SHRIMP, cooked, chopped	3 quarts
CELERY, finely chopped	3 cups
GREEN ONIONS, finely chopped	¾ cup
MAYONNAISE	¾ cup
SALT	1 teaspoon
DILL WEED	1 teaspoon
LEMON JUICE	2½ tablespoons
MUSTARD, dry	4 teaspoons
BUTTER or MARGARINE, softened	1 pound
LEMON RIND, grated	2 teaspoons
BREAD	29 slices

Procedure

1. Drain pineapple. Measure required amount of syrup.

2. Beat pineapple syrup with lemon juice, oil, salt and sugar. Pour over drained pineapple slices; chill several hours.

3. Combine shrimp, celery and onion. Blend mayonnaise with salt, dill, lemon juice and mustard. Pour over shrimp mixture; mix lightly but well. Chill.

4. Mix butter and lemon rind.

5. To assemble each sandwich; spread bread with lemon butter; cover with shrimp filling; top with pineapple slice. Garnish with additional shrimp (whole), if desired.

MUSHROOM BEEF BURGERS
(See picture, p. 80)

Try garnishing with halved cherry tomatoes in a nest of chicory.

Yield: 48 portions

Ingredients

MUSHROOMS, fresh	2 pounds
or	
MUSHROOM STEMS AND PIECES, canned	1½ quarts
BEEF, lean, ground	12 pounds
ONIONS, finely chopped	2 cups
SALT	3 to 4 tablespoons
MUSTARD, powdered	3 tablespoons
PEPPER, black, ground	2 teaspoons
INSTANT GARLIC POWDER	1 teaspoon
ITALIAN BREAD SLICES	48
MUSHROOM GRAVY*	2 gallons

Procedure

1. Rinse, pat dry and chop fresh mushrooms (makes about 3 quarts). Or, drain canned mushrooms.

2. Combine mushrooms with meat, onions, and seasonings. Mix lightly but thoroughly. Do not overmix.

3. Shape into individual patties. Broil or grill until done as desired.

4. To serve, place each patty on a slice of Italian bread. Spoon hot mushroom gravy over all. Garnish as desired. Serve at once.

*MUSHROOM GRAVY

Yield: 2 gallons

Ingredients

MUSHROOMS, fresh	2 pounds
or	
MUSHROOMS, sliced, canned	2 1-pound cans
SALAD OIL	½ cup
BROWN SAUCE or PREPARED BEEF GRAVY	3 quarts
TOMATO SAUCE	2 quarts
INSTANT ONION POWDER	2 teaspoons
INSTANT GARLIC POWDER	1 teaspoon
SALT	as needed
PEPPER, black, ground	as needed

Procedure

1. Rinse, pat dry and slice fresh mushrooms (makes 2½ quarts). Or, drain canned mushrooms.

2. Saute mushrooms in oil until golden.

3. Stir in remaining ingredients; heat thoroughly. Check seasoning, adding salt and pepper as needed.

WESTERN CHEESE BUNS

Round out the plate with french fried potatoes, a bouquet of cress and a crisp celery heart.

Yield: 100 portions

Ingredients

CHEESE, cheddar, shredded	6¼ pounds
GREEN PEPPER, chopped	½ pound (1¾ cups)
ONION, chopped	1 pound (2 cups)
STUFFED OLIVES, chopped	2 cups
CHILI SAUCE	2½ cups
SANDWICH BUNS, sliced	100

Procedure

1. Blend cheese, green pepper, onion, olives and chili sauce.
2. Toast buns. Spread bottom halves with cheese mixture allowing 1/3 cup per bun.
3. Place under a low broiler or in a 350°F. oven until cheese is melted.
4. Cover with top halves of toasted buns.

DUTCH TREAT PLATE

Try completing the menu with cream of cauliflower soup and with a peanut brittle sundae for dessert.

Yield: 1 portion

Ingredients

HAM, sliced tissue thin	2½ ounces
CRACKED WHEAT BUN, lightly buttered	1
DUTCH POTATO SALAD	1 No. 10 scoop
LETTUCE CUP	1
CHEESE, American	1½ slices
HOLLAND DRESSING*	1 ounce

Procedure

1. Heap ham on bottom half of bun. Handle lightly. Place top slightly off side. Do not cut or press. Place on one side of plate.
2. Arrange potato salad in lettuce cup on other side of plate.
3. Cut slices of cheese diagonally. Place triangles upright against potato salad.
4. Add souffle cup of dressing.

*To make Holland dressing, combine equal amounts of mayonnaise, prepared mustard and sweet pickle relish.

United Fresh Fruit and Vegetable Assn.

SALADS

WITH TODAY'S keen interest in "lighter" meals, entree salads can put your luncheon and supper menus in tune with the times. Now, regardless of season, salad meals are "in." And the smiles of satisfaction they will bring reflect their cool, refreshing looks and all-round good taste.

There's a wide variety of salads substantial enough to be an adequate main dish. The list includes the adaptable chicken, turkey and seafood salads, as well as rib-sticking mixtures based on meat, eggs, cooked vegetables and cheese. Besides, there are any number of sturdy additions that will transform tossed green salads into meal-making chef's salad bowls.

The collection of salad recipes that makes up this chapter embraces salads in loaves to serve forth in slices and an aspic pie to cut into wedges. There are mixtures to present in crisp pastry shells or to pile into hollowed-out pineapple halves. And others to arrange within a frame of brittle-crisp greens.

Bread, in some form, is a natural companion. Dainty sandwiches, an herbed loaf, crusty rolls or a piping hot quick bread can fill the role. Add a steaming portion of soup or a frosty juice (if you will) and offer a dessert that completes the harmony of your salad meal.

TUNA SALAD
Add a portion of potato chips to round out the offering.

Yield: 100 portions (No. 12 scoop)

Ingredients

TUNA, solid pack, drained	10½ pounds
CHEESE, cheddar, grated	2½ pounds
PINEAPPLE CUBES or TIDBITS, drained	1½ No. 10 cans
ONION, grated	½ cup
MUSTARD, dry	2 tablespoons
MAYONNAISE	1½ quarts

Procedure

1. Flake tuna; combine with cheese and pineapple.
2. Stir onion and mustard into mayonnaise, blending well. Pour over tuna mixture; toss lightly to mix. Chill.
3. Serve on crisp greens.

ORANGE-SHRIMP MACARONI SALAD
Arrange with chilled cooked broccoli spears, lightly coated with oil and lemon juice dressing. For flavor contrasts, serve a caramel custard for dessert.

Yield: 24 portions

Ingredients

ORANGES, fresh, peeled, cut into bite-size pieces	6 large
or	
MANDARIN ORANGES, drained	1-1/2 quarts
SHRIMP, cooked	1-1/2 pounds
MACARONI, shell or elbow, cooked	1-1/2 quarts
CELERY, diced	1-1/2 cups
ONION, finely chopped	3/4 cup
MAYONNAISE	1-1/2 cups
MUSTARD, prepared	1 tablespoon
SALT	3/4 teaspoon
PEPPER, black (coarse grind)	1/8 teaspoon
LETTUCE CUPS	24
LEMON WEDGES	24

Procedure

1. Combine oranges, shrimp, macaroni, celery and onion; toss to mix.
2. Combine mayonnaise, mustard, salt and pepper; blend. Pour over macaroni mixture; toss to mix. Chill.
3. Serve in lettuce cups. Garnish with lemon wedges.

CHICKEN OR TURKEY SALAD

Serve with slices of premise-made Melba toast and top off the meal with a slice of chocolate-frosted devil's food cake.

Yield: 50 ¾-cup portions

Ingredients

SALAD DRESSING	3 cups
SALT	1 tablespoon
CHICKEN or TURKEY, cooked, cut into cubes	5 quarts
CELERY, chopped	2 quarts
CUCUMBER, chopped	1½ quarts
EGGS, hard-cooked, chopped	16
ALMONDS, sliced, toasted	3 cups

Procedure

1. Blend salad dressing and salt. Add to chicken; mix lightly.
2. Add celery, cucumber and eggs; toss lightly. Check seasoning, adding more salt, if necessary.
3. Serve on crisp greens. Top with almonds.

KIDNEY BEAN AND FRANKFURTER SALAD

Toasted English muffins go well with this hearty salad. For a full-fledged meal, you might add a cup of tomato bouillon and a fruit dessert—sliced peaches, a ripe pear, or a grapefruit half.

Yield: 32 portions

Ingredients

KIDNEY BEANS, drained	1 No. 10 can
FRANKFURTERS, sliced	2 pounds
EGGS, hard-cooked, chopped	12
SWEET PICKLES, chopped	2 cups
CELERY, chopped	1 quart
GREEN PEPPER, chopped	1 cup
ONION, finely chopped	½ cup
SALT	1 tablespoon
PEPPER	1 teaspoon
MAYONNAISE or SALAD DRESSING	4½ cups

Procedure

1. Combine kidney beans, frankfurters, eggs, pickles, celery and green pepper.
2. Add onion, salt and pepper to mayonnaise; mix well. Pour dressing over salad mixture; toss lightly to mix. Chill.

HAM PINEAPPLE LUNCHEON SALAD

Scones or hot biscuits are crisp companions for this salad; complete menu listing with a custard-filled eclair.

Yield: 50 portions

Ingredients

SALAD OIL	1 cup
LEMON JUICE	¼ cup
SALT	½ teaspoon
PEPPER	¼ teaspoon
MUSTARD	¼ teaspoon
HAM, cooked, cut in small cubes	5 quarts
CELERY, sliced	2½ quarts
PINEAPPLE TIDBITS, drained	1¼ quarts
PECANS, coarsely chopped	2½ cups
SALAD DRESSING	3 cups
PINEAPPLE JUICE	¼ cup
MARJORAM	½ teaspoon

Procedure

1. Make a French dressing of salad oil, lemon juice, salt, pepper and mustard.
2. Combine with ham. Marinate in refrigerator for at least two hours.
3. Add celery, pineapple and pecans to ham.
4. Combine salad dressing, pineapple juice and marjoram. Pour over ham mixture; toss lightly. Refrigerate until ready to serve.
5. Serve on crisp salad greens.

VEGETABLE POTATO SALAD

This colorful vegetable salad can make wonderful alliances with cold cuts, sliced cheese or chilled sardines.

Yield: 2½ gallons;60 2/3-cup portions

Ingredients

DEHYDRATED SLICED POTATOES	1 package (2-1/4 pounds)
SALT	1/4 cup
WATER	2 gallons
CUT GREEN BEANS, cooked, drained	2 quarts
CARROTS, cooked, diced, drained	2 quarts
CELERY, diced	2 quarts
PARSLEY, chopped	1 quart (12 ounces)
MAYONNAISE	1-1/4 quarts
ONION, grated	1/3 cup
LEMON JUICE	1/3 cup
SALT	2-1/2 tablespoons
PEPPER	1-1/2 teaspoons
SOUR CREAM	1 quart

Procedure

1. Cook potatoes with salt and water as directed on package. Drain well. Add vegetables and parsley. Cool.

2. Mix mayonnaise, seasonings and sour cream. Pour over vegetables; toss lightly. Chill.

3. Serve on crisp salad greens. Top with a slice of hard-cooked egg and a sprinkling of chopped parsley, if desired.

TOMATO ASPIC PIE WITH VEGETABLE CHEESE TOPPING

A new and different item to use as the basis for an exciting cold plate. For dessert, suggest a pear half a la mode with chocolate sauce.

Yield: 6 9-inch pies

Ingredients

GELATIN, LEMON FLAVOR	1½ pounds
SALT	2 tablespoons
CAYENNE	½ teaspoon
TOMATO JUICE, hot	2 quarts
TOMATO JUICE, cold	2½ quarts
HORSERADISH, prepared	3 tablespoons
ONION, grated	3 tablespoons
PIE SHELLS, 9-inch, baked	6
VEGETABLE COTTAGE CHEESE*	4½ pounds
CHIVES or PARSLEY, chopped (optional)	as needed

Procedure

1. Combine gelatin, salt and cayenne. Add hot tomato juice; stir until gelatin is dissolved.

2. Add cold tomato juice, horseradish and onion. Chill until well thickened.

3. Pour into pie shells, allowing about 3 cups per shell. Chill until firm.

4. Spread with vegetable cottage cheese allowing 12 ounces per pie. Garnish with chopped chives or parsley, if desired.

5. Serve wedges as a salad cold plate (with shelled cooked shrimp, potato chips, olives, etc.).

*VEGETABLE COTTAGE CHEESE

Yield: 4½ pounds

Ingredients

CUCUMBERS, finely diced	1 pound
RADISHES, sliced	3/4 cup
GREEN ONIONS, finely chopped	1/3 cup
CELERY, finely chopped	1-1/2 cups (6 ounces)
GREEN PEPPERS, finely chopped	1 cup
COTTAGE CHEESE	2½ pounds
SALT	1-1/2 teaspoons
MAYONNAISE	1/4 cup

SALMON OR TUNA MOLD

Add "extras" of sliced cucumbers, carrot curls and tender young scallions. Add pamper your dessert lovers with pecan waffles topped with ice cream and butterscotch sauce.

Yield: 1½ gallons

Ingredients

GELATIN, unflavored	2-1/2 ounces (1/2 cup)
WATER, cold	1-1/2 cups
MILK, hot	3 quarts
VINEGAR	1-1/2 cups
MAYONNAISE	3 cups
SUGAR	1/4 cup
SALT	2 tablespoons
LIQUID HOT PEPPER SEASONING	1 teaspoon
MUSTARD, dry	1-1/2 tablespoons
SALMON or TUNA, flaked	3 pounds
CELERY, finely cut	3 cups
ONION, grated chopped	1/3 cup
OLIVES, stuffed	1 cup

Procedure

1. Soften gelatin in cold water 5 minutes. Add to hot milk; stir until gelatin is dissolved. Cool.

2. Add vinegar, mayonnaise, sugar, salt, liquid hot pepper seasoning and mustard. Chill until slightly thickened.

3. Fold in remaining ingredients. Turn into individual molds or loaf pans. Chill until firm.

4. Unmold or slice. Serve on crisp salad greens.

▼   ▼

Procedure

1. Combine vegetables, cottage cheese, salt and mayonnaise; mix lightly but well.

2. Chill thoroughly.

SALAD OF THE SOUTH SEAS

Croissants team well with this lamb-and-fruit item. And Boston cream pie is a pleasing choice as a dessert suggestion.

Yield: 24 portions

Ingredients

LAMB, cooked, cut julienne	6 pounds
CELERY, sliced diagonally	1½ quarts
MANDARIN ORANGE SEGMENTS, drained	3 quarts
PINEAPPLE CUBES, drained	3 quarts
COCONUT	1½ cups
MAYONNAISE	1 quart
CURRY POWDER	¼ cup
LETTUCE or other crisp greens	as needed

Procedure

1. Combine lamb, celery, oranges, pineapple and coconut; toss lightly.
2. Mix mayonnaise and curry powder, blending well.
3. For each portion, line a salad bowl with greens; mound 1½ cups lamb salad on the greens. Top with approximately 2 tablespoons curried mayonnaise.

SPORTSMAN'S LAMB SALAD

Piping hot buttermilk biscuits provide crisp contrast for this hearty salad. And rhubarb pie can fill the bill when it comes to dessert.

Yield: 24 portions

Ingredients

LAMB, cooked, cubed	6 pounds
ONION RINGS	1½ quarts
ITALIAN DRESSING	3 cups
CHEESE, American, cut julienne	1½ pounds
SALAD PICKLES, drained	1½ quarts
LETTUCE, or other crisp greens	as needed
TOMATOES, cut in wedges	24
FRENCH DRESSING	3 cups

Procedure

1. Marinate lamb cubes and onion rings in Italian dressing for one hour.
2. Combine lamb, onion rings, cheese and pickles; toss lightly.
3. For each portion, arrange 1½ cups lamb salad mixture on greens. Garnish with tomato wedges allowing one tomato for each salad. Serve with 2 tablespoons French dressing.

Salad of the South Seas (top);
Sportsman's Lamb Salad (below)

American Lamb Council

COLD MEAT FESTIVAL SALAD

A sturdy main-dish salad designed to please the keenest appetite. Let it star on a menu that begins with apricot nectar and ends with maple walnut ice cream and a frosted cake square.

Yield: 1½ gallons

Ingredients

MUSTARD, powdered	1 tablespoon
WATER	1 tablespoon
INSTANT CHOPPED ONION	1/3 cup
WATER	1/3 cup
SALT	2 tablespoons
PEPPER, ground black	1 teaspoon
INSTANT GARLIC POWDER	1/4 teaspoon
MAYONNAISE	3/4 to 1 cup
LEMON JUICE	1 tablespoon
MACARONI, elbow, cooked	2-1/2 quarts
RED KIDNEY BEANS, canned	1 quart
HAM, TONGUE or LUNCHEON MEAT, cooked, diced	1 quart
CELERY, diced	1-1/2 quarts
SALAD GREENS	3 quarts
PAPRIKA	as needed

Procedure

1. Mix mustard with first amount of water; let stand 10 minutes.

2. Mix instant chopped onion with remaining water; let stand 10 minutes.

3. Combine hydrated mustard and onion with salt, pepper, garlic powder, mayonnaise and lemon juice; mix well.

4. Combine macaroni, red kidney beans, meat and celery in a large mixing bowl. Add mayonnaise mixture; toss lightly to mix. Refrigerate at least 1 hour.

5. Serve on salad greens. Garnish with paprika.

CRAB LOUIS

A West Coast favorite that customers welcome, wherever they are. The popular accompaniment: crisp-crusted rolls or sour dough bread.

Yield: 24 portions

Ingredients

LETTUCE LEAVES	as needed
ICEBERG LETTUCE, shredded	as needed
CUCUMBERS, sliced	2 to 3
EGGS, hard-cooked, quartered	12
KING CRAB MEAT, chunks	5 pounds
CRAB LOUIS DRESSING*	1½ quarts

Procedure

1. Line shallow salad bowl with lettuce leaves; mound shredded lettuce in center.

2. Arrange approximately 3 ounces crab meat on top, cucumber slices and 2 egg quarters at the side.

3. Drizzle with dressing.

*CRAB LOUIS DRESSING

Yield: 1½ quarts

Ingredients

MAYONNAISE	3 cups
CREAM, heavy	3/4 cup
CHILI SAUCE	3/4 cup
WORCESTERSHIRE SAUCE	1 tablespoon
GREEN PEPPER, minced	3/4 cup
ONION, minced	3/4 cup
LEMON JUICE	1/3 cup

Procedure

Combine ingredients; chill.

JELLIED EGG SALAD

For added elegance, serve with a dressing of equal parts mayonnaise and sour cream with caviar or tiny shrimp folded in.

Yield: 32 4-ounce portions

Ingredients

GELATINE, unflavored	2 ounces (6 tablespoons)
WATER, cold	1-1/2 cups
MILK, hot	2-1/2 cups
EGGS, hard-cooked, coarsely cut	30
GREEN PEPPERS, chopped	1 cup
CELERY, finely cut	3-1/2 cups
SALT	2 tablespoons
MAYONNAISE	2 cups
SOUR CREAM	1/2 cup
PIMIENTOS, chopped	1 cup
PICKLE RELISH, drained	3/4 cup
LEMON JUICE	2/3 cup

Procedure

1. Soak gelatine in cold water 5 minutes. Add hot milk gradually; stir until gelatine is dissolved. (If milk starts to curdle, place over cold water and beat with rotary beater until smooth.) Chill until slightly thickened.

2. Fold in remaining ingredients.

3. Turn into loaf pans. Chill until firm.

4. Unmold; cut into slices. Serve on crisp salad greens with mayonnaise. Garnish with tomato wedges and ripe olives, if desired.

CRABMEAT RICE SALAD

Present with a sprightly assortment of relishes and a basket of rolls. Be prepared to offer lemon or lime chiffon pie as a dessert.

Yield: 2 gallons; 48 2/3-cup portions

Ingredients

MAYONNAISE	1½ quarts
LEMON JUICE	3 tablespoons
SALT	2½ tablespoons
PEPPER	1½ teaspoons
RICE, cooked, hot	2¼ quarts
CRABMEAT*	2¼ quarts
CELERY, diced	2¼ quarts
FROZEN GREEN PEAS, cooked, cooled	2½ quarts
PIMIENTO, diced	¾ cup

ROCK LOBSTER SALAD SUPREME

Companionable menu items include marinated asparagus, crisp radishes and seeded rolls.

Yield: 2 gallons

Ingredients

INSTANT POTATO SLICES	1 2¼-pound package
ROCK LOBSTER, cooked, diced*	2 quarts
EGGS, hard-cooked, chopped	4
CELERY, chopped	1 cup
CUCUMBER, quartered, sliced	1 cup
MAYONNAISE	1¼ quarts
VINEGAR, cider	2 tablespoons
ONION, grated	¼ cup
SALT	2 tablespoons
GREEN PEPPER, finely chopped	¼ cup
PARSLEY, chopped	1 tablespoon

Procedure

1. Prepare potato slices according to package directions. Drain. Cool.
2. Combine potatoes, lobster, eggs, celery and cucumber.
3. Blend mayonnaise, vinegar, onion, salt, green pepper and parsley. Pour over potato mixture; toss lightly to mix. Chill.

*To prepare frozen South African lobster tails; cover with water; bring just to a boil. Reduce heat; simmer about 5 minutes. Pour off water. When cool enough to handle, cut through tails lengthwise with kitchen shears; peel away skin and tendons. Carefully remove meat from shell. Dice coarsely.

Procedure

1. Mix mayonnaise, lemon juice, salt and pepper.
2. Add to hot cooked rice; toss lightly to mix. Cool.
3. Add crabmeat, celery, peas and pimiento; toss together lightly. Chill about 1 hour to blend flavors before serving.
4. Serve on crisp salad greens. Garnish with tomato wedges.

*Cooked diced chicken, lobster or shrimp may be substituted. With chicken, reduce lemon juice to 2 tablespoons.

CURRIED SEAFOOD AND PINEAPPLE SALAD

An impressive salad that can set off a round of favorable comment when presented in a fresh pineapple shell or within a framework of perky, crisp greens.

Yield: 48 portions

Ingredients

INSTANT MINCED ONION	1 cup
WATER	1 cup
HALIBUT, cooked, flaked	5 pounds
SHRIMP, cooked, peeled, deveined, diced	4 pounds
TUNAFISH, drained, flaked	2 pounds
OIL and VINEGAR DRESSING	2 cups
PINEAPPLE, fresh*	24 small
EGGS, hard-cooked, diced	12
MAYONNAISE	2 quarts
CURRY POWDER	½ cup
LEMON JUICE	3 tablespoons
SALT	4 teaspoons
WHITE PEPPER, ground	1 teaspoon
PARSLEY FLAKES	¼ cup
SHRIMP, cooked, peeled, deveined, cut lengthwise into halves	24

Procedure

1. Combine minced onion and water; let stand 10 minutes to rehydrate.

2. Combine halibut, shrimp and tuna; add rehydrated onion. Pour oil and vinegar dressing over mixture; toss to mix. Let marinate 10 minutes.

3. Halve pineapples lengthwise cutting through leaves and keeping them intact. With a sharp knife cut along underside of core and around edge of shell to loosen edible part of fruit. Scoop out the flesh of the pineapple; core and dice.

4. Drain fish mixture. Add diced pineapple and egg.

5. Combine mayonnaise, curry powder, lemon juice, salt and pepper; mix well. Add to fish; toss gently.

6. Spoon mixture into pineapple shells. Garnish with parsley flakes and half a shrimp.

*If desired, use 1 No. 10 can pineapple wedges, drained, in place of fresh pineapple. Serve mixture on crisp salad greens.

CHINESE SHRIMP SALAD

Toasted walnuts give this entree salad a distinctive touch. To carry out the menu in an Oriental vein, add sweet potato rolls and a creamy tapioca pudding topped with sliced preserved kumquats.

Yield: 24 portions

Ingredients

BUTTER or MARGARINE	3 tablespoons
SOY SAUCE	3 tablespoons
WALNUT HALVES	3 cups
SHRIMP, cooked, deveined	2¼ quarts
CELERY, sliced diagonally	3 cups
GREEN PEPPER, diced	1 cup
PINEAPPLE CHUNKS, drained	3 cups
SWEET SOUR DRESSING*	as needed

Procedure

1. Melt butter; add soy sauce and walnuts. Stir gently over low heat until walnuts are toasted. Remove from pan. Cool.
2. Cut each shrimp in half lengthwise.
3. Combine shrimp, celery, green pepper and pineapple. Add sweet-sour dressing to moisten ingredients.
4. Fold in walnuts.
5. Serve on crisp salad greens allowing ¾ cup mixture per portion. Serve with additional dressing, if desired.

*SWEET-SOUR DRESSING

Yield: 2¼ quarts

Ingredients

SUGAR	1½ cups
SALT	3 tablespoons
MUSTARD, dry	2 tablespoons
CORNSTARCH	1 tablespoon
PEPPER, white, ground	¼ teaspoon
CAYENNE	dash
VINEGAR	3 cups
SALAD OIL	1½ quarts

Procedure

1. Combine dry ingredients in a tall kettle with tight-fitting lid. (Use tall kettle to avoid boiling over.)
2. Add vinegar; heat, stirring occasionally, until mixture boils. Cover; reduce heat. Boil exactly 5 minutes. Cool.
3. Add salad oil slowly beating with a whip.
Note: Dressing separates on standing. Before using, beat to mix thoroughly.

TUNA AND WHITE GRAPE SALAD IN PASTRY SHELLS

Present with a cranberry juice cocktail, corn muffins and butterscotch pudding garnished with pecans.

Yield: 50 portions

Ingredients

TUNAFISH	6 13-ounce cans
CELERY, sliced	2½ quarts
THOMPSON SEEDLESS GRAPES	1½ quarts
GREEN PEPPER, shredded	1½ cups
MAYONNAISE	3 cups
PAPRIKA	1 tablespoon
MUSTARD, dry	1 tablespoon
SALT	2 teaspoons
LEMON JUICE	½ cup
PASTRY TART SHELLS, baked	50
CHICORY	as needed

Procedure

1. Flake tuna.   Combine with celery, grapes and green pepper.
2. Combine mayonnaise, paprika, mustard, salt and lemon juice; mix well.
3. Pour dressing over tuna mixture; toss lightly to mix.   Chill.
4. Serve in pastry shells. Garnish with chicory or watercress.

FRIZZLED BEEF SALAD BOWL

Try accompanying this salad bowl with small sandwiches made with a snappy cheese spread and offer an ice cream pie with fruit sauce by way of dessert.

Yield: 24 portions

Ingredients

DRIED BEEF	1½ pounds
BUTTER or MARGARINE	¼ pound
MIXED SALAD GREENS, torn in pieces	1½ gallons
CAULIFLOWER	1 medium head
CARROTS, raw, thinly sliced	1 pound
PEAS, cooked	2 cups
GREEN PEPPER, quartered, sliced	6 ounces
CELERY SEED	¾ teaspoon
TOMATOES, cut in wedges	3 pounds
EGGS, hard-cooked, sliced	4

COTTAGE CHEESE SALAD LOAF

Tomatoes and ripe and/or green olives make a tasty garnish for this salad. For other go-alongs, try toasted corn muffins and blueberry pie.

Yield: 1½ gallons mixture; 48 ½-cup portions

Ingredients

GELATINE, unflavored	2½ ounces
MILK	3½ quarts
SALT	3 tablespoons
CAYENNE	½ teaspoon
VINEGAR	1 cup
ONION, grated	2 tablespoons
COTTAGE CHEESE	2 quarts
GREEN PEPPER, chopped	1 cup
PIMIENTO, chopped	1 cup
PECANS, cut* (optional)	1 cup

Procedure

1. Sprinkle gelatine on milk; let stand 5 minutes. Add salt and cayenne; heat to dissolve gelatine.

2. Cool. Add vinegar and onion. Chill until slightly thickened.

3. Fold in remaining ingredients. Pour into loaf pans; chill until firm. Unmold. Slice; serve on crisp salad greens.

*Cut, do not chop pecans for this recipe, small bits of chopped nuts give a greyish cast to the loaf.

Procedure

1. Cut or tear apart pieces of dried beef.

2. Melt butter in heavy skillet; add beef; saute until edges frizzle and curl.

3. Combine greens, cauliflower, carrots, peas, green pepper and celery seed. Toss with frizzled beef.

4. Fill individual salad bowls; garnish with tomato wedges and egg slices. Serve with oil and vinegar dressing.

TARTAR SALAD

Sesame wafers make a pleasing accompaniment. Chicken noodle soup and coconut bread pudding can complete the meal.

Yield: 36 portions

Ingredients

SALAD OIL	2¼ cups
VINEGAR	¾ cup
MUSTARD, prepared	¼ cup
SALT	3 tablespoons
BLACK PEPPER, ground	1 teaspoon
ROAST BEEF, cooked, cut in strips	6 pounds
GREEN BEANS, cut, cooked	1½ quarts
DILL PICKLES, chopped	1½ cups
PIMIENTO SLICES, undrained	6 2-ounce jars
ONIONS, chopped	1 cup
EGGS, hard-cooked, cut in wedges	12
LETTUCE	as needed
EGGS, hard-cooked, cut in wedges	6
PARSLEY or WATERCRESS	as needed

Procedure

1. Combine salad oil, vinegar, mustard, salt and pepper; beat or shake until well mixed.

2. Combine beef, green beans, pickles, pimiento, and onions. Add dressing; toss lightly to mix. Add first amount of eggs; toss lightly.

3. Pile on lettuce leaves. Garnish with remaining eggs and parsley or watercress.

CHICKEN SALAD TARTS VERONIQUE

To round out the menu, add oven-warm Parkershouse rolls and chocolate pudding a la mode.

Yield: 24 portions

Ingredients

ALMONDS, sliced natural	2½ cups
CHICKEN MEAT, cooked, cubed	3 quarts (4 pounds)
GRAPE S, whole white seedless or halved, seeded red grapes	1½ quarts
CELERY, sliced	3 cups
PINEAPPLE CHUNKS, fresh, frozen or canned, drained	3 cups
MAYONNAISE	3 cups
SOUR CREAM	3 cups
LEMON JUICE	½ cup
HORSERADISH	½ cup
CELERY SEED	2½ teaspoons
SALT	1 teaspoon
PASTRY TART SHELLS, baked	24

Procedure

1. Spread almonds evenly in a shallow pan. Place in a 350°F. oven 3 minutes or until lightly toasted. Cool. Reserve about 1/3 of the almonds for garnish.

2. Combine remaining almonds, chicken, grapes, celery and pineapple.

3. Combine mayonnaise, sour cream, lemon juice, horseradish, celery seed and salt; mix.

4. Pour dressing over chicken mixture; toss lightly to mix.

5. Portion salad mixture in pastry shells allowing about ¾ cup per portion. Sprinkle tops with reserved almonds. Serve with a whole spiced peach, 2 sherried ripe olives and spears of romaine, if desired.

SEAMAN'S SALAD

A salad bowl that packs a bonus of taste and eye appeal. Try combining with cream of spinach soup, crisp crackers and sliced peach pie with a lattice top.

Yield: 25 portions

Ingredients

LETTUCE LEAVES, crisp	as needed
LETTUCE, torn	1 pound, 9 ounces
FISH FILLETS, poached, cooled, broken into chunks	8 pounds
PEAS, cooked	2½ pounds
CARROTS, thinly sliced	2 pounds
RADISHES, thinly sliced	1 bunch
TOMATO WEDGES	75
FAIR-WEATHER DRESSING*	1½ quarts

Procedure

1. Line salad bowls with lettuce leaves. Mound about 1 ounce torn lettuce in center.
2. Arrange 5 ounces, chilled, cooked chunks of fillets on top.
3. Garnish with 1½ ounces cooked peas, 1¼ ounces carrot slices, thin radish slices and 3 tomato wedges.
4. Serve with fair weather dressing.

*FAIR-WEATHER DRESSING

Yield: 1½ quarts

Ingredients

MAYONNAISE	3 cups
SOUR CREAM	3 cups
MUSTARD, prepared	2 tablespoons
CURRY POWDER	1½ teaspoons

Procedure

1. Combine ingredients; mix.
2. Chill thoroughly, allowing time for flavors to blend.

CHEF'S SALAD BOWL

A salad bowl that ventures away from the beaten path. Try featuring with a crusty whole grain bread. Or, with king-size hot popovers, for a sprightly change.

Yield: 24 portions

Ingredients

SUMMER SAUSAGE, cut in julienne strips	1½ pounds
SMOKED BEEF TONGUE, cut in julienne strips	1½ pounds
LETTUCE, in bite-size pieces	1½ gallons
WATERCRESS	2 cups
CHICORY, escarole or spinach	2 quarts
TOMATOES, medium, cut into wedges	6
EGGS, hard-cooked, cut into eighths	12
CHEESE, American or Swiss, cubed	12 ounces
FRENCH DRESSING	2 cups

Procedure

1. Combine meat, greens, tomatoes, eggs and cheese; mix lightly.
2. Just before serving, add dressing; toss lightly to mix.

SHRIMP, RICE AND LIMA SALAD

This colorful salad gains extra appeal from cloverleaf rolls and a punch cup of pink rhubarb sauce with shortbread cookies.

Yield: 24 portions

Ingredients

RICE, cooked	1½ quarts
SHRIMP, cooked, cut in pieces	1½ quarts
LIMA BEANS, green, cooked	1 quart
CELERY, sliced	1 quart
FRENCH DRESSING	1½ cups
SALT	1 tablespoon
DILL, fresh, chopped	2 tablespoons
or	
DRIED DILL	1½ teaspoons

Procedure

1. Combine rice, shrimp, lima beans, celery, French dressing, salt and dill. Toss lightly to mix. Chill.
2. Serve on crisp salad greens. Garnish with additional fresh dill, if desired.

American Dairy Association

POULTRY

THE AMERICAN regard for poultry still keeps its luster though the birds once held in reserve for a special occasion are now a mealtime treat for any day of the year.

With the changing times, marketing practices are vastly different than in yesteryear. Items such as poultry-in-parts and the cooked chicken and turkey meat which comes in several forms have inspired the creation of many new dishes. And they have made scores of old favorites a cinch to prepare.

Chicken and turkey marry well with other foods. They are in harmonious company with a variety of vegetables and a number of fruits. Both meats have a delicate flavor that can stand on its own, though they can readily accept a cautious addition of spices or herbs and even go so far as to agree with the hot, pungent taste of a barbecue sauce.

In the main, the collection of recipes presented here is designed to satisfy hearty appetites, please simple tastes and yet in no way slight the palate of the sophisticates. To lovers of chicken and turkey dishes, bon appetit!

BRUNSWICK STEW

Serve with crisp crackers or hot crusty bread and offer a small green salad and a gelatin dessert.

Yield: 24 portions

Ingredients

CHICKEN PARTS	8 pounds
BEEF SHIN, boneless	3 pounds
PORK SPARERIBS	3 pounds
WATER, cold	1 gallon
SALT	3 tablespoons
BLACK PEPPER, whole	1 teaspoon
CRUSHED RED PEPPER	½ teaspoon
POTATOES, diced	2 quarts
GREEN BEANS, cut ½-inch	1 quart
PEAS	1 quart
OKRA, cut 1-inch	1 quart
LIMA BEANS, green	1 quart
KERNEL CORN	2 cups
TOMATOES	1 No. 10 can
ONION FLAKES	2 cups
BLACK PEPPER, ground	1 teaspoon
BUTTER or MARGARINE	4 ounces

Procedure

1. Combine chicken, beef, pork, water, salt, whole pepper and crushed red pepper. Cover; cook slowly until meat falls from bones. Remove bones; discard.

2. Cut chicken and meat into cubes; return to stock.

3. Add vegetables, onion flakes and ground black pepper. Cook slowly 30 minutes, stirring occasionally.

4. Add butter; remove from heat.

SWEET AND SOUR PINEAPPLE TURKEY

Chinese pea pods make a nice "go-along."

Yield: 24 portions

Ingredients

CARROTS, peeled, sliced	3 cups
CHICKEN STOCK	1½ quarts
CELERY, sliced diagonally	3 cups
ONION, cut in 1-inch squares	3 cups
STOCK FROM COOKING VEGETABLES	3 cups
PINEAPPLE SYRUP (from canned pineapple chunks)	3 cups
SOY SAUCE	1/4 cup
SUGAR, light brown (packed measure)	1/4 cup
CORNSTARCH	1/3 cup
CATSUP	1/2 cup
VINEGAR	6 tablespoons
TURKEY, cooked, cut in strips	1-1/2 quarts
CANNED PINEAPPLE CHUNKS, drained	1-1/4 quarts
GREEN PEPPER, cut in 1-inch squares	3 cups

Procedure

1. Cook carrots in chicken stock 5 minutes.

2. Add celery and onion; cook 5 minutes longer. Drain, reserving required amount of stock.

3. Combine reserved stock with pineapple syrup, soy sauce and sugar.

4. Blend cornstarch with catsup; add to liquid mixture. Cook and stir until sauce clears and thickens.

5. Add vinegar, turkey, pineapple chunks, green pepper and cooked vegetables. Heat through.

6. Serve with hot rice.

WESTERN BARBECUE CHICKEN

Celery hearts, ripe olives and hot brown-crusted corn sticks are well-suited companions for this tasty dish.

Yield: 25 portions

Ingredients

CHICKEN BREASTS OR LEGS WITH THIGHS, large	25
COOKING OIL	as needed
SALT	as needed
PEPPER	as needed
CRUSHED PINEAPPLE WITH SYRUP	1½ quarts
CATSUP	2 cups
VINEGAR	½ cup
SUGAR, light brown	½ cup (packed)
WORCESTERSHIRE SAUCE	2 tablespoons
MUSTARD, dry	1 teaspoon
GARLIC SALT	¼ teaspoon

Procedure

1. Arrange chicken in baking pan. Brush with oil. Season with salt and pepper.
2. Bake in 350°F. oven 45 minutes.
3. Combine remaining ingredients, simmer 20 minutes.
4. Pour pineapple sauce over chicken. Continue baking 15 to 20 minutes or until chicken is done.

CHICKEN 'N BISCUIT PIE

A homey dish with unlimited appeal. Try featuring with a chopped cabbage and celery seed relish in a sugar-vinegar dressing. Ice cream with strawberry sauce makes a companionable dessert.

Yield: 21 to 22 portions

Ingredients

ONION, chopped	1/2 cup
SHORTENING	1 tablespoon
CREAM OF CHICKEN SOUP, condensed	1 50-ounce can
MILK	2 cups
CHICKEN, cooked, diced	2 pounds
POTATOES, diced, cooked	1 pound
CARROTS, diced, cooked	8 ounces
PEPPER, black	1/8 teaspoon
RICH BISCUIT DOUGH	2-1/2 pounds

TURKEY AND RICE BARBECUE

A pungent barbecue sauce snaps up the mild flavor of turkey roll.

Yield: 50 portions

Ingredients

ONIONS, finely chopped	1-1/2 quarts (2 pounds)
SHORTENING	1 cup (7 ounces)
MUSTARD, dry	3 tablespoons
SUGAR, brown	1 cup (6 ounces)
BEEF SOUP BASE	1/2 cup (4 ounces)
CATSUP	2 quarts
WATER	1 quart
VINEGAR	1-1/2 cups
WORCESTERSHIRE SAUCE	1/3 cup
HOT PEPPER SAUCE	1/2 teaspoon
TURKEY ROLL, sliced,heated	6-1/4 pounds
RICE, cooked, hot	2 gallons

Procedure

1. Simmer onions in shortening until lightly browned.

2. Add mustard, brown sugar, soup base, catsup, water, vinegar, Worcestershire sauce and hot pepper sauce. Simmer until sauce is of desired consistency, about 20 to 30 minutes.

3. To serve, arrange hot turkey on rice allowing 2 ounces turkey and 2/3 cup rice per portion. Spoon on 1/3 cup sauce.

▼ ▼

Procedure

1. Cook onion in shortening until tender.

2. Blend in soup and milk; stir until smooth.

3. Add chicken, potatoes, carrots and pepper; heat.

4. Pour into 12-inch by 18-inch by 2-inch baking pan or 22 individual casseroles (2/3 cup in each).

5. Top with a rich biscuit crust cut to fit baking pan or casseroles.

6. Bake in a 425°F. oven 20 to 30 minutes or until sauce is bubbling and crust is done.

SHERRIED CELERY AND CHICKEN ORIENTAL

Try rounding the menu with a green salad bowl and baked coconut custard.

Yield: 48 portions

Ingredients

OIL, peanut or salad	1 cup
CELERY, sliced diagonally	3 gallons
ONIONS, sliced	1 gallon
MUSHROOMS, sliced	2 quarts
GARLIC, finely minced	2 teaspoons
CHICKEN STOCK	3 cups
SOY SAUCE	2 cups
SHERRY, dry	1 cup
SUGAR	½ cup
GINGER, ground	2 tablespoons
SALT	4 teaspoons
PEPPER, black, ground	1 teaspoon
CORNSTARCH	½ cup
WATER, cold	½ cup
CHICKEN, cooked, julienne or diced	1 gallon
RICE, cooked, hot	2 gallons

Procedure

1. Heat oil in large heavy skillet or saucepan. Add celery, onions, mushrooms and garlic; saute 8 to 10 minutes, stirring occasionally.

2. Add stock, soy sauce, sherry, sugar, ginger, salt and pepper. Bring to boiling point; cook, stirring frequently, for 10 minutes.

3. Blend cornstarch with cold water; stir into celery mixture. Add chicken; continue cooking 5 to 8 minutes or until celery is crisp tender.

4. Serve over hot rice.

Sherried Celery and Chicken Oriental

The Florida Celery Advisory Committee

CHICKEN DIVAN

An imaginative chicken and vegetable combination. Fresh pineapple or strawberries and cookies make a congenial dessert.

Yield: 50 portions

Ingredients

BUTTER or MARGARINE	1½ pounds
FLOUR	1 pound, 2 ounces
PEPPER, white	¾ teaspoon
CHICKEN SOUP BASE	3 ounces (6 tablespoons)
WATER, boiling	1½ gallons
DESSERT TOPPING MIX, prepared*	3 quarts
PARMESAN CHEESE, grated	6 ounces (1½ cups)
ASPARAGUS or BROCCOLI SPEARS, frozen, cooked	7½ pounds
CHICKEN, cooked, sliced	6¼ pounds
PARMESAN CHEESE, grated	6 ounces (1½ cups)

Procedure

1. Melt butter. Add flour, pepper and soup base; blend well.
2. Stir in boiling water. Cook and stir until thickened.
3. Mix in whipped topping and first amount of Parmesan cheese.
4. Place cooked vegetable in shallow pan; cover with half of the sauce. Arrange chicken on top; cover with remaining sauce.
5. Sprinkle with remaining cheese. Place under broiler until cheese is melted and golden brown.

*Prepare topping without sugar and vanilla.
Variations: Make with turkey or ham in place of chicken.

COUNTRY CAPTAIN

A dish with East Indian flavor that has deep roots in our southland. As one story has it, the recipe was introduced to Georgia by a sea captain who was involved in the spice trade.

Yield: 24 portions

Ingredients

CHICKEN, half breasts, thighs and drumsticks	18 pounds
SALT	2 tablespoons
PEPPER	1 teaspoon
COOKING OIL	as needed
ONIONS, chopped	1½ cups
GREEN PEPPER, chopped	1 cup
GARLIC, crushed	2 to 3 cloves
CURRY POWDER	1/3 cup
THYME	1 tablespoon
TOMATOES, seasoned, stewed	3 quarts
CURRANTS or RAISINS	1 cup
RICE, cooked, hot	1 gallon
ALMONDS, blanched, toasted	1½ cups
CHUTNEY	as needed

Procedure

1. Season chicken pieces with salt and pepper.
2. Brown chicken in oil in heavy skillet over moderate heat.
3. Remove chicken from skillet; add onion, green pepper, garlic, curry powder and thyme. Cook until onion is tender but not brown.
4. Add stewed tomatoes, currants and chicken. Cover; simmer 20 to 30 minutes or until chicken is tender.
5. Spoon over rice, sprinkle with almonds. Serve with chutney.

CHICKEN SUPREME

Try presenting with whipped potatoes and/or whole green beans sprinkled with bacon bits. Offer peach halves a la mode with just-thawed red raspberries for dessert.

Yield: 25 6-ounce portions, 2 ounces sauce

Ingredients

CHICKEN PARTS	10 pounds
or	
READY-TO-COOK FRYING CHICKENS	
minus backs and necks	12 pounds
FLOUR, sifted	2 cups
SALT	1 tablespoon
PAPRIKA	1 teaspoon
PEPPER	½ teaspoon
BUTTER or MARGARINE, melted	4 ounces
CREAM OF MUSHROOM SOUP	1 50-ounce can
MILK	1 cup

Procedure

1. Coat chicken pieces in mixture of flour and seasonings. Arrange in single layer in greased baking pans.
2. Brush generously with melted butter.
3. Bake in a 400°F. oven for 30 minutes. Turn chicken; bake another 30 minutes.
4. Blend soup and milk; pour over chicken. Return to oven; continue to bake until sauce is bubbly hot, about 10 minutes.

SCALLOPED TURKEY AND STUFFING ═══════

Plate with baked sweet potatoes and a jellied cranberry salad.

Yield: 48 portions

Ingredients

BUTTER or MARGARINE	½ pound
ONION, finely chopped	2 cups
BREAD CUBES, soft, ½-inch	2½ gallons
SALT	4 teaspoons
PEPPER	½ teaspoon
SAGE	2 teaspoons
BUTTER or MARGARINE	½ pound
FLOUR	1 pound
NONFAT DRY MILK	1 cup
CHICKEN BROTH	4¾ quarts
PEAS, canned or frozen	2 quarts
TURKEY ROLL, diced	6 pounds

SESAME FRIED CHICKEN BREASTS

Scalloped potatoes team well with this chicken dish and broiled peach halves make an effective garnish.

Yield: 24 portions

Ingredients

EGGS, beaten	3
MILK	1½ cups
FLOUR	3 cups
BAKING POWDER	1 tablespoon
SALT	2 tablespoons
PAPRIKA	2 tablespoons
PEPPER	¾ teaspoon
CHICKEN BREASTS, split	7½ pounds (24 pieces)
BUTTER	¾ pound
SESAME SEEDS	6 tablespoons

Procedure

1. Combine eggs and milk.
2. Sift flour, baking powder, salt, paprika and pepper to thoroughly mix.
3. Dip chicken breasts in egg and milk mixture, then into the flour mixture.
4. Melt butter in a 12-inch by 20-inch shallow pan. As pieces of floured chicken are placed in pan, turn to coat with butter. Turn, skin side down in a single layer; sprinkle with sesame seeds.
5. Bake in a 400°F. oven 25 minutes. Turn chicken, sprinkle with sesame seeds; bake another 20 minutes, or until tender.

▼ ▼

Procedure

1. Melt first amount of butter. Add onion; simmer until tender.
2. Combine bread cubes, salt, pepper and sage in a 3-gallon mixing bowl. Add onion-butter mixture; mix well.
3. Melt remaining butter; blend in flour. Sift nonfat dry milk into mixture; blend.
4. Add chicken broth gradually, blending after each addition. Cook and stir until thickened. Fold in peas and turkey.
5. Arrange a layer of stuffing in each of 2 greased 12-inch by 20-inch by 2-inch steam table pans, using ¼ of the stuffing per pan.
6. Divide ½ of the turkey mixture over the stuffing in the two pans.
7. Add another layer of stuffing and another of the turkey mixture.
8. Bake in a 350°F. oven 30 minutes.

RAISIN CHICKEN CALIFORNIA

A taste-tempting dish to present with rice.

Yield: 25 portions

Ingredients

FLOUR	1/3 cup
SEASONED SALT	2 tablespoons
PAPRIKA	2 teaspoons
CHICKEN BREASTS, large*	25 (about 10-3/4 pounds)
OIL, cooking	1/2 cup
MANDARIN ORANGES	2 1-pound, 14-ounce cans
CHICKEN BROTH	3 cups
VINEGAR	2/3 cup
CORNSTARCH	2-3/4 ounces
CHICKEN BROTH	3/4 cup
RAISINS, dark seedless	10 ounces
MARASCHINO CHERRIES, whole, drained	1 cup
MARASCHINO CHERRY SYRUP	1/2 cup

Procedure

1. Mix flour, seasoned salt and paprika. Coat chicken lightly with seasoned flour.

2. Pour oil in baking pan. Arrange chicken pieces in pan, skin side down. Bake in a 450°F. oven 20 minutes.

3. Turn pieces of chicken skin side up; continue baking 15 minutes or until tender.

4. Drain oranges, reserving syrup. Combine syrup, first amount of broth and vinegar; heat to boiling.

5. Blend cornstarch with remaining broth; stir into the hot liquid, continuing to cook and stir until thickened and clear.

6. Add raisins, cherries and cherry syrup; simmer 5 minutes. Add drained oranges; heat through. Serve sauce over chicken.

Note: If sauce is to be held, add oranges just before serving.

*Or chicken legs with thighs attached.

CREAMED CHICKEN AND MUSHROOMS DUCHESSE

To complete the menu, present with a salad of greens tossed with orange sections and avocado; and for dessert, slices of cream-filled chocolate roll.

Yield: 48 portions

Ingredients

POTATOES, peeled	20 pounds
BUTTER	¾ pound
SALT	¼ cup
WHITE PEPPER, ground	1 teaspoon
NUTMEG, ground	1 teaspoon
EGGS	12
BUTTER	½ pound
ONIONS, minced	2 cups
MUSHROOMS, sliced	3 quarts
CHICKEN, cooked, diced	1½ gallons
CREAM SAUCE	1 gallon
SHERRY	½ cup
BUTTER, melted	¼ pound
PARSLEY	as needed

Procedure

1. Cook potatoes. Mash thoroughly or put through a ricer. Add first amount of butter, salt, pepper and nutmeg.

2. Add eggs, one at a time, beating well after each addition.

3. Melt next amount of butter in a large pot. Add minced onions and sliced mushrooms. Saute lightly over low heat.

4. Add diced chicken and cream sauce. Bring to a boil. Add sherry; simmer 10 minutes. Check seasoning.

5. Using a pastry bag, pipe potato mixture to form a nest inside individual casseroles. Drizzle ½ teaspoon of the melted butter on top of potato in each casserole. Brown lightly under a very slow broiler.

6. Ladle about ¾ cup hot creamed chicken in center of each casserole. Garnish with parsley.

SCALLOPED CHICKEN AND NOODLES

Green peas with small white onions complements this entree. And a fruit cup or fruit salad can round out the meal.

Yield: 50 1-cup portions

Ingredients

CHICKEN, cooked, boned	4¾ pounds
NOODLES, medium	2¼ pounds
WATER, boiling	1 gallon
SALT	¼ cup
CHICKEN FAT AND BUTTER	2 pounds
FLOUR	1 pound, 2 ounces
PEPPER	1 tablespoon
NONFAT DRY MILK	1¼ pounds
CHICKEN STOCK, cold	1 quart
CHICKEN STOCK, hot	1¾ gallons
BREAD CRUMBS, soft	4 ounces
CHEESE, grated	8 ounces

Procedure

1. Cut chicken in large pieces.

2. Cook noodles in boiling salted water until tender. Drain. Rinse in cold water.

3. Melt chicken fat and butter. Remove from heat. Blend in flour, pepper and nonfat dry milk. Mix until smooth.

4. Add cold chicken stock; beat to a smooth paste. Gradually add hot chicken stock. Cook and stir over low heat until thickened and smooth.

5. Divide sauce into two parts. Add chicken to one part, noodles to the other.

6. Spread noodle mixture over bottom of two 12-inch by 20-inch baking pans. Spread chicken mixture evenly on top.

7. Mix bread crumbs and cheese; sprinkle on top.

8. Bake in a 375°F. oven 30 minutes or until heated through and crumbs are brown.

TURKEY A LA QUEEN

For a bonus of good taste, make white sauce with half cream and half chicken or turkey broth and add a well beaten egg yolk for each quart of sauce.

Yield: 50 ¾-cup portions

Ingredients

TURKEY, cooked, cubed	5 pounds
MEDIUM WHITE SAUCE, hot	1¼ gallons
PINEAPPLE TIDBITS, drained	3 pounds
CHOW MEIN NOODLES	3 pounds
ALMONDS, slivered, sauteed	½ pound

Procedure

1. Add turkey to white sauce. Keep hot over hot water for 1 hour to blend flavors.
2. Add pineapple. Serve over noodles. Top with almonds.

ORANGE BARBECUED CHICKEN WINGS

Rice is a natural escort for this dish.

Yield: 20 portions

Ingredients

CHICKEN WINGS, large	60
SALT	as needed
SHORTENING or COOKING OIL	as needed
ORANGE JUICE, freshly squeezed	2 quarts
ORANGES, peeled, cut in bite-size pieces	2 quarts
TOMATO SAUCE	2 quarts
SUGAR, light brown	½ cup (packed)
WORCESTERSHIRE SAUCE	½ cup
INSTANT MINCED UNION	3 tablespoons
MUSTARD, dry	1 tablespoon
LIQUID HOT PEPPER SEASONING	¼ teaspoon

Procedure

1. Sprinkle chicken wings with salt. Brown in shortening. Arrange in steamtable pans, 1 layer deep.
2. Combine remaining ingredients; mix well. Pour over chicken.
3. Bake in 375°F. oven 40 to 45 minutes or until done.

American Dairy Association

FISH and SEAFOOD

COOKS around the world have innumerable ways with fish and seafood. This small collection of recipes, selected for you, includes ideas for preparing a variety of the different kinds of fish and shellfish that are available in most of this country's markets—fresh, frozen or canned.

Some of the dishes are simple and homey, others unusual, and a few are, quite frankly, on the elaborate side. Each boasts of distinction in its own special way. Almost all of them are quick and easy to make.

Fish with its quick-cooking feature meets one of the needs that is prevalent today. But this is an advantage that's far too seldom recognized and understood. Fish is by nature a delicate, tender product and needs only a small amount of heat to render it done. Once beyond that point it starts to get overly firm, begins to dry out and toughen.

Fish is done when it "flakes." Or, in other words, when probing it with a fork at the thickest part, the flesh slides easily at its natural divisions or "markings." As another clue, both fish and shellfish are done as soon as the flesh becomes opaque and no longer has a shiny look.

Learning to recognize the just-done stage so you can present your fish dishes at their prime can assuredly win a whole new round of enthusiastic friends!

BAKED FISH PATTIES

This homey dish combines well with a colorful salad of mixed cooked vegetables and squares of devil's food cake, topped with ice cream.

Yield: 48 portions

Ingredients

POTATOES, cooked, hot	8 pounds
BUTTER or MARGARINE	½ pound
PARSLEY FLAKES	½ cup
SALT	3 tablespoons
WHITE PEPPER	2 teaspoons
NUTMEG	1 teaspoon
EGGS	8
FISH, cooked, flaked	10 pounds

Procedure

1. Mash potatoes. Add butter, parsley flakes, salt, pepper and nutmeg.
2. Add eggs, one at a time, beating well after each addition. Add flaked fish.
3. Refrigerate mixture until cool.
4. Shape on floured board into 3-ounce patties. Place on greased baking sheet.
5. Bake in 375°F. oven 30 minutes or until lightly browned.
6. Serve 2 patties per portion with curried tomato sauce* (facing page) or herbed egg sauce.**

**HERBED EGG SAUCE

Yield: 48 portions

Ingredients

MUSTARD, powdered	2 tablespoons
WATER, warm	2 tablespoons
CREAM SAUCE, rich	2½ quarts
PARSLEY FLAKES	¼ cup
DEHYDRATED CHIVES	¼ cup
INSTANT ONION POWDER	1 tablespoon
EGGS, hard-cooked, diced	12

Procedure

1. Mix mustard with warm water; let stand 10 minutes for flavor to develop.
2. Heat cream sauce, stirring constantly. Add mustard and remaining ingredients.

DEVILED SEAFOOD SPECIAL

Try featuring with individual loaves of freshly baked bread and a salad bowl of greens tossed with halved, cooked Brussels sprouts.

Yield: 24 ½-cup portions

Ingredients

GREEN PEPPER, chopped	1 quart
CELERY, finely chopped	1 quart
ONION, finely chopped	1½ tablespoons
MUSTARD, dry	1½ tablespoons
WORCESTERSHIRE SAUCE	1½ tablespoons
SALT	2 teaspoons
PEPPER	½ teaspoon
SHRIMP, cooked	1¾ pounds
CRABMEAT, cooked, flaked	1¾ pounds
SALAD DRESSING	1 quart
BREAD CRUMBS, soft, buttered	1 quart

Procedure

1. Combine ingredients except buttered crumbs; toss to mix well.
2. Portion ½ cup mixture into individual seafood shell or casserole. Top with crumbs.
3. Bake in a 350°F. oven 30 minutes.

---

*CURRIED TOMATO SAUCE

Yield: 48 portions

Ingredients

TOMATO SAUCE	3 quarts
CURRY POWDER	½ cup

Procedure

1. Heat tomato sauce.
2. Add curry powder; mix well. Allow sauce to stand several minutes for flavors to blend.

SALMON MOUSSELINE

Serve on plate with hash brown potato shreds and a bouquet of cress.

Yield: 24 portions, approximately 6 ounces, 1½ ounces sauce

Ingredients

SALMON, canned, skin and bones removed	4 pounds
EGG WHITES	1 cup
SALT	2 tablespoons
PEPPER, white	½ teaspoon
TARRAGON, dried, finely crumbled	1¼ teaspoons
CREAM, heavy	2 quarts
TOMATO PASTE	¾ cup
RIPE OLIVES, coarsely chopped	3 cups
PARSLEY, chopped	½ cup
MORNAY SAUCE*	4½ cups

Procedure

1. Grind salmon using fine blade of grinder. Chill thoroughly.
2. Place ground salmon in mixer bowl. Beat in egg whites gradually. Add salt, pepper and tarragon.
3. Blend in cream slowly, mixing thoroughly.
4. Add tomato paste; mix well. Stir in olives and parsley.
5. Fill greased timbale molds with mixture, allowing 6 ounces per portion. Set in steam table pan, add hot water to half depth of molds.
6. Bake in a 350°F. oven 20 to 25 minutes, until firm.
7. Unmold; cover each portion with 1½ ounces Mornay sauce.

*MORNAY SAUCE

Yield: 4½ cups

Ingredients

BUTTER or MARGARINE	2 ounces
FLOUR	6 tablespoons
SALT	1-1/2 teaspoons
PEPPER, white	1/8 teaspoon
MILK, scalded	1 quart
LIQUID RED PEPPER SEASONING	1/16 teaspoon
PARMESAN CHEESE, grated	1 cup

Procedure

1. Combine butter and flour. Cook together slowly 3 to 4 minutes.
2. Add salt, pepper and hot milk. Cook and stir until sauce boils and thickens.
3. Add red pepper seasoning and cheese; heat slowly until cheese melts and sauce is smooth.

BAKED SALMON LOAF

Offer with cut green beans, a cucumber salad and a choice of desserts.

Yield: 48 portions

Ingredients

MILK, scalded	3 cups
BREAD CRUMBS, soft	2 quarts
EGGS, slightly beaten	12
SALMON, flaked	10 pounds
LEMON JUICE	½ cup
BUTTER or MARGARINE, melted	¼ pound
PARSLEY FLAKES	½ cup
SALT	2 tablespoons
INSTANT ONION POWDER	4 teaspoons
PAPRIKA	4 teaspoons
MUSTARD, powdered	2 teaspoons
WHITE PEPPER	1½ teaspoons

Procedure

1. Pour scalded milk over bread crumbs in a large mixing bowl. Gradually add eggs and remaining ingredients, blending well.

2. Divide mixture into 6 greased 4-inch by 9-inch loaf pans.

3. Set pans in tray containing one inch of water. Bake in a 325°F. oven 1¼ hours or until lightly browned and firm to the touch.

4. Let loaves stand 20 minutes before slicing. Serve with creamed mushroom sauce.*

*CREAMED MUSHROOM SAUCE

Yield: 48 portions

Ingredients

CREAM SAUCE, rich	3 quarts
INSTANT ONION POWDER	4 teaspoons
MUSHROOMS, sliced	1½ quarts
BUTTER or MARGARINE, melted	¼ pound
CREAM, light	1 cup
SHERRY	½ cup
PARSLEY FLAKES	¼ cup

Procedure

1. Heat cream sauce, stirring constantly. Add onion powder.

2. Saute mushrooms in butter until lightly browned.

3. Add mushrooms, light cream, sherry and parsley flakes to cream sauce. Bring to boiling point, stirring constantly. Remove from heat at once.

4. Serve over sliced salmon loaf.

INDIVIDUAL SCALLOP CASSEROLES

Serve with a combination of rice and peas, an artichoke heart salad and a canned fruit compote (pear half, whole peeled apricot and dark sweet cherries).

Yield: 24 portions

Ingredients

SCALLOPS	8 pounds
EGG YOLKS, slightly beaten	4
CREAM, light	2 cups
DRY WHITE WINE	1 cup
LEMON JUICE	2 tablespoons
INSTANT CHOPPED ONION	3 tablespoons
WHITE PEPPER, ground	½ teaspoon
GINGER, ground	½ teaspoon
SALT	1 tablespoon
BREAD CRUMBS, soft	1 quart
BUTTER or MARGARINE, melted	½ cup
CHEESE, PARMESAN, grated	½ cup

Procedure

1. Arrange scallops in individual coquille shells or baking dishes. (If scallops are large, cut in bite-size pieces.)

2. Combine beaten egg yolks, cream, wine, lemon juice and seasonings; mix well. Pour equal amounts (about 2 tablespoons) of mixture over each portion of scallops.

3. Combine bread crumbs, melted butter and cheese. Sprinkle over scallops. Bake in 425°F. oven 10 to 12 minutes or until scallops are done and topping browned. Do not allow sauce to boil.

BAKED FISH FILLETS WITH PUFFY CHEESE SAUCE ═══════

Scalloped potatoes go well with this dish, as does a jellied tomato aspic with cucumber mayonnaise.

Yield: 100 portions

Ingredients

HADDOCK FILLETS*, fresh or frozen	18 pounds
MAYONNAISE or SALAD DRESSING	2-1/2 cups
PICKLE RELISH, drained	1/2 cup
CHEESE, grated	2 cups (8 ounces)
EGG YOLKS, beaten	2/3 cup (8)
SALT	2 tablespoons
EGG WHITES	1 cup (8)

FRESH BROCCOLI AND TUNA AU GRATIN

Present with an assortment of relishes and freshly baked rolls. For dessert, offer coffee ice cream with crushed peanut brittle.

Yield: 24 portions

Ingredients

BUTTER or MARGARINE	6 ounces
FLOUR	3 ounces (¾ cup)
MILK	1½ quarts
SALT	1 tablespoon
BLACK PEPPER, ground	½ teaspoon
CHEDDAR CHEESE, sharp, grated	½ pound
LEMON JUICE	3 tablespoons
BROCCOLI, fresh	6 pounds
TUNA FISH, flaked	1 pound, 12 ounces
BREAD CRUMBS, soft	1½ quarts
BUTTER or MARGARINE, melted	8 ounces

Procedure

1. Melt first amount of butter; blend in flour.
2. Gradually stir in milk. Cook and stir over low heat until thickened and smooth.
3. Blend in seasonings, cheese and lemon juice. Set aside, keeping warm.
4. Cook broccoli until crisp tender. Drain.
5. Arrange broccoli in baking pans or individual serving dishes.
6. Top with tuna fish; spread with cheese sauce.
7. Combine crumbs and melted butter; toss and mix. Sprinkle over cheese sauce.
8. Bake in 350°F. oven 30 minutes.

▼ ▼

Procedure

1. Thaw frozen fillets. Divide into 100 portions, about 2½ ounces each. Place in a single layer in well-greased baking pans.
2. Combine mayonnaise, relish, cheese, egg yolks and salt.
3. Beat egg whites until stiff; fold into mayonnaise mixture.
4. Cover fish with the sauce.
5. Bake in a 350°F. oven about 30 minutes or until the fish flakes easily when tested with a fork and sauce is brown.

*Or cod, flounder, ocean perch, pollock, rockfish, whiting or yellow perch fillets.

SCALLOPED TUNA AND POTATOES AU GRATIN

Try pairing this easy-to-make tuna dish with a sliced tomato and green pepper ring salad. Star Dutch apple pie with warm lemon sauce in the role of dessert.

Yield: 50 portions

Ingredients

INSTANT SLICED POTATOES	1 2¼-pound package
FLOUR	1½ cups (6 ounces)
SALT	2 tablespoons
PEPPER, white	½ teaspoon
ONIONS, finely chopped	1 cup
PIMIENTO, diced	¼ cup
TUNA FISH, drained, flaked	4¼ pounds
NONFAT DRY MILK, reconstituted, hot	2 quarts
WATER, hot	3½ quarts
CHEESE, CHEDDAR, grated	2 pounds

Procedure

1. Place half of the potatoes, as they come from the package, into a 12-inch by 20-inch by 4-inch baking pan.
2. Combine flour, salt and pepper. Sprinkle over potatoes.
3. Layer onions, pimiento and tuna fish on top.
4. Cover with remaining potatoes.
5. Pour on hot milk and hot water; mix thoroughly.
6. Bake, uncovered in a 400°F. oven for 30 minutes.
7. Mix in cheese. Bake 30 minutes longer or until potatoes are tender.

GLOUCESTER SHRIMP RAREBIT

To complete the menu scheme, try adding a vegetable juice cocktail, cucumber and watercress salad and Dutch apple cake.

Yield: 24 portions—1 slice toast; 5 shrimp; ½ cup sauce

Ingredients

MARGARINE	8 ounces
FLOUR	1 cup (4 ounces)
LIQUID WHOLE MILK	2¼ quarts
CHEESE, PASTEURIZED PROCESS, cubed	1½ pounds
WORCESTERSHIRE SAUCE	2 teaspoons
MUSTARD, dry	1 tablespoon
PEPPER	½ teaspoon

TUNA CHOP SUEY

One or two preserved kumquats make a nice addition to the plate and cool wedges of melon provide an appealing dessert.

Yield: 2 gallons, 50 portions; 2/3-cup chop suey, 1/2-cup rice

Ingredients

CELERY, cut in strips	3 quarts
ONIONS, sliced	2 quarts
GREEN PEPPERS, coarsely chopped	1 quart
SHORTENING	7 ounces (1 cup)
LIQUID FROM BEAN SPROUTS PLUS WATER	3 quarts
SALT	4 teaspoons
QUICK COOKING TAPIOCA	1 to 1-1/3 cups
SOY SAUCE	1/2 to 2/3 cup
TUNA, drained, coarsely flaked	4 pounds
BEAN SPROUTS, well drained	8 ounces (2 cups)
RICE, hot cooked	1-1/2 gallons

Procedure

1. Cook celery, onions and peppers in shortening about 5 minutes. Do not overcook. Vegetables should be crisp.
2. Drain liquid from bean sprouts. Add hot water to make required amount of liquid. Add to vegetables with salt, tapioca and soy sauce.
3. Cook, covered, 5 minutes, stirring occasionally.
4. Add tuna and bean sprouts. Simmer a few minutes to heat.
5. Serve on rice. Garnish with toasted almonds or crisp noodles, as desired.

SHRIMP, freeze-dried, prepared as directed on label*	120
TOAST SLICES, cut in quarters	24

Procedure

1. Make a white sauce with margarine, flour and milk. Add cheese and seasonings, stirring until cheese is melted.
2. For each portion, arrange 5 shrimp in an individual casserole. Cover with ½ cup cheese sauce. Heat in a 400°F. oven. Arrange 4 toast points on top.

*Or, shirmp, large, cooked.

TUNA STROGANOFF

Try featuring with a marinated cooked vegetable salad and red cherry crunch with almond custard sauce.

Yield: 14 portions

Ingredients

LEMON JUICE from	2 lemons
TUNA, drained, flaked	1½ pounds
ONIONS, finely minced	2 cups
MARGARINE	½ pound
FLOUR	¼ cup
TOMATO PASTE	1¼ cups
WATER	3¼ cups
GARLIC POWDER	½ teaspoon
SALT	2 teaspoons
WORCESTERSHIRE SAUCE	1 tablespoon
SUGAR	¾ cup
PAPRIKA	1½ teaspoons
SOUR CREAM (dairy)	3 cups
RICE, cooked	1½ quarts

Procedure

    1. Sprinkle lemon juice over drained tuna.

    2. Saute onions in margarine 5 minutes; add flour; blend.

    3. Add tomato paste, water, garlic powder, salt, Worcestershire sauce, sugar and paprika; blend; bring to a boil.

    4. Add tuna; heat through. Add sour cream; blend but do not boil.

    5. Serve 6 ounces tuna stroganoff in casserole; top with a No. 12 scoop cooked rice. Garnish with parsley. Place casserole on hot dinner plate for service.

BAKED FISH ON TOMATO-PARMESAN STUFFING

This combines well with whole kernel corn and a fruited gelatin dessert with topping or cream.

Yield: 48 portions

Ingredients

BREAD CUBES, ½-inch, soft	3½ pounds
MARJORAM or SAGE	1½ teaspoons
ONION, instant minced	1 tablespoon
PARMESAN CHEESE, grated	¾ pound
CREAM OF TOMATO SOUP, condensed	1 50-ounce can
BUTTER or MARGARINE, melted	1 pound
SALT	1 tablespoon
FISH FILLETS or STEAKS, fresh or frozen, thawed (3-ounces each)	48
PAPRIKA	1½ teaspoons

Procedure

1. Combine bread cubes, marjoram, onion and cheese in a mixing bowl. Toss with 2 large forks to blend ingredients.

2. Add undiluted soup and 1-1/3 cups of the butter, blending with the same forks.

3. Place half of the stuffing in each of 2 greased 12-inch by 20-inch by 2½-inch steam table pans, spreading stuffing evenly in pans.

4. Arrange 24 pieces of fish over stuffing in each pan. (If fillets have skin, place skin side down.)

5. Add paprika to remaining butter; brush evenly over fish.

6. Cover pans; bake in a 350°F. oven 40 minutes or until fish flakes easily with a fork and flesh has lost its shiny, transparent look. Do not overcook.

Note: If thick fish steaks are used, increase baking time about 15 minutes.

FISH PORTIONS MORNAY

Try presenting with french fried potatoes and offering raspberry sherbet for dessert.

Yield: 32 portions

Ingredients

FISH PORTIONS, precooked (3-ounce)	32 (1 6-pound box)
GREEN BEANS, French style, canned	2½ No. 10 cans
or	
GREEN BEANS, French-style, frozen, cooked	4½ 40-ounce packages
PIMIENTO, diced	2 cups
BUTTER or MARGARINE	1 pound
SALT	as needed
PEPPER	as needed
GARLIC POWDER	as needed
CHEESE SAUCE, hot	3 quarts

Procedure

1. Bake fish portions in a 400°F. oven for approximately 12 minutes.
2. Heat canned green beans; drain. Or, cook frozen beans; drain.
3. Divide beans evenly into 4 12-inch by 20-inch by 2-inch pans. Add ½ cup pimiento and ¼ pound butter to each pan. Toss lightly to mix.
4. Arrange hot fish portions on top of beans.
5. Serve portions topped with 1/3 cup cheese sauce.

CRAB BISCAYNE

A good combination with leaf spinach and Fordhook lima beans.

Yield: 48 ½-cup portions

Ingredients

CATSUP	3 cups
VINEGAR	¾ cup
BUTTER or MARGARINE, melted	4 ounces
WORCESTERSHIRE SAUCE	¼ cup
SALT	1 teaspoon
LIQUID HOT PEPPER SEASONING	½ teaspoon
CRAB MEAT, flaked	6 pounds
EGGS, hard-cooked, chopped	24
BREAD CRUMBS, soft	1½ quarts
CHEESE, American process, grated	1 pound

ALASKA KING CRAB QUICHE

A menu special with a lightly dressed green salad fashioned of tender, small lettuce leaves; crusty bread; a ripe pear, and Camembert or Brie cheese.

Yield: 6 9-inch quiche

Ingredients

KING CRAB MEAT	1½ quarts
ONIONS, chopped, sauteed	1½ cups
CHEESE, Swiss, grated	3 cups
PASTRY LINED 9-INCH PIE PANS	6
EGGS	24
HALF AND HALF	2 quarts
VERMOUTH, dry	¾ cup
LEMON JUICE	½ cup
MUSTARD, dry	1 tablespoon
CAYENNE	¼ teaspoon
SALT	1 to 1½ tablespoons

Procedure

1. Divide crab meat, onions and cheese evenly into pie shells.
2. Beat eggs, half and half, vermouth, lemon juice and seasonings until blended. Fill shells with mixture.
3. Bake in a 350°F. oven 45 minutes or until custard is browned and set.
4. Cut in wedges. Serve warm.

Procedure

1. Combine catsup, vinegar, butter, Worcestershire, salt and hot pepper seasoning.
2. Gently mix in crab meat, eggs and crumbs.
3. Place mixture in individual shells or casseroles allowing ½ cup mixture per portion. Top with cheese.
4. Bake in 375°F. oven 20 minutes or until cheese melts and mixture is hot.

CHEESED MASHED POTATOES WITH BROILED FILLET

A happy combination of potatoes and fish that goes well with sliced pickled beets arranged on cress and squares of gingerbread with lemon sauce.

Yield: 12 portions

Ingredients

FISH FILLETS, fresh or frozen	3 pounds
POTATOES, mashed, seasoned	1½ quarts
EGGS, slightly beaten	2
CHEESE, CHEDDAR, shredded	8 ounces (2 cups)
ONION, finely chopped	¼ cup
CHEESE, CHEDDAR, shredded	4 ounces (1 cup)
BUTTER, melted	2 ounces (¼ cup)
SALT	as needed
PEPPER, white	as needed
PAPRIKA	as needed
LEMON WEDGES	12

Procedure

1. Thaw fish, if frozen. Drain well. Cut fillets into 12 4-ounce portions.

2. Combine mashed potatoes, eggs, first amount of shredded cheese and onion; beat until well blended.

3. Divide potato mixture into 12 individual casseroles. Sprinkle with remaining cheese. Bake in a 350°F. oven 15 to 20 minutes.

4. Brush fillets with melted butter. Sprinkle with salt, pepper and paprika. Broil 8 to 10 minutes or until fish flakes when tested with a fork.

5. Top each casserole with a broiled fillet. Serve with lemon wedge.

Cheesed Mashed Potatoes with Broiled Fillet

POLYNESIAN SHRIMP AND PINEAPPLE

To round out a menu that echoes the Islands, combine with buttered Chinese pea pods and a coconut dessert.

Yield: 24 portions

Ingredients

PINEAPPLE CHUNKS	1 No. 10 can
PINEAPPLE JUICE	1 1-quart, 14-ounce can*
VINEGAR	1½ cups
SOY SAUCE	½ cup
CORNSTARCH	¾ cup
GINGER, ground	1 teaspoon
WATER	½ cup
SUGAR, brown	6 ounces
SALT	as needed
GREEN PEPPER, cut into strips	12 ounces
ONION RINGS	1½ pounds
SHRIMP, cooked, peeled	3 pounds

Procedure

1. Drain pineapple chunks, reserving syrup.
2. Combine pineapple syrup, pineapple juice, vinegar and soy sauce. Bring to a boil.
3. Blend cornstarch and ginger with water; stir into hot liquid. Cook and stir until thickened. Add sugar; stir until dissolved. Season with salt. Keep warm.
4. Combine just before serving. For each 2 portions, add ¾ cup pineapple chunks, 1 ounce green pepper strips. 2 ounces onion rings and 4 ounces shrimp to 8 ounces sauce. Cook 1 minute to heat through. Serve over rice.

*Or, ½ No. 10 can.

ESCALLOPED TUNA, EGGS AND OLIVES

Feature with buttered crisp-tender zucchini, an orange, grapefruit and avocado salad, and thick slices of a crusty whole-grain bread.

Yield: 50 6-ounce portions

Ingredients

TUNA, canned	5 pounds
MILK and TUNA LIQUID	1 gallon
BUTTER or MARGARINE	12 ounces
FLOUR	5 ounces (1¼ cups)
SALT	2 tablespoons
STUFFED OLIVES, sliced	2 cups
EGGS, hard-cooked	5 dozen
BUTTER or MARGARINE, melted	6 ounces
BREAD CRUMBS	1 quart
PARMESAN CHEESE, grated	6 ounces

Procedure

1. Drain tuna, reserving the liquid for making the cream sauce. Flake tuna.

2. Heat milk and tuna liquid together.

3. Melt butter; blend in flour. Add hot liquid; cook and stir until thickened. Add salt.

4. Carefully fold tuna and sliced olives into sauce.

5. Quarter eggs; arrange in two 12-inch by 20-inch by 2½-inch steam table pans. Cover with creamed tuna mixture dividing equally between the two pans.

6. Mix melted butter, bread crumbs and Parmesan cheese. Sprinkle over top of each pan.

7. Bake in 350°F. oven 20 to 25 minutes or until thoroughly heated through and top is browned.

BAKED HALIBUT IN SOUR CREAM

A popular menu choice served with new potatoes browned in butter, asparagus tips, and angel food cake with a lemon glaze.

Yield: 24 5-ounce portions

Ingredients

HALIBUT STEAKS, cut 3 to the pound	24
SALT	as needed
SOUR CREAM	2 quarts
ONIONS, finely chopped	1 cup
DILL PICKLES, finely chopped	1 cup
PARSLEY, chopped	½ cup
PIMIENTO, chopped	½ cup
MUSTARD, dry	2 teaspoons
BASIL, dried	2 teaspoons
LEMON JUICE	½ cup
PARMESAN CHEESE, grated	¼ cup

Procedure

1. Arrange steaks in a well oiled baking pan.
2. Sprinkle lightly with salt.
3. Combine sour cream, onions, pickles, parsley, pimiento, mustard, basil and lemon juice. Spread mixture evenly over the halibut steaks.
4. Sprinkle with Parmesan cheese.
5. Bake in a 375°F. oven for 25-30 minutes.

SCALLOPS MARSEILLES

Arrange with buttered broccoli spears and cooked diagonally cut celery for an eye-catching plate.

Yield: 60 portions

Ingredients

SCALLOPS, fresh or frozen	15 pounds
BUTTER or MARGARINE	1 pound
ONION, finely chopped	5 ounces
FLOUR	1 pound
MILK, hot	1¼ gallons
SALT	3 tablespoons
CAYENNE	½ to 1 teaspoon
TOMATO PASTE	8 ounces
CREAM, light	3 cups
SHERRY	1 cup

SHERRIED SEAFOOD

As a change-about, try serving over green noodles. Or, alongside a mix-ture of brown and white rice.

Yield: 25 ½-cup portions

Ingredients

CRAB MEAT, cut in 1-inch pieces	1¼ pounds
SCALLOPS, cooked	1¼ pounds
SHRIMP, cooked, deveined	1¼ pounds
BUTTER or MARGARINE	9 ounces
FLOUR	4½ ounces
PAPRIKA	1 tablespoon
SALT	1½ teaspoons
CAYENNE	¼ teaspoon
MILK, hot	1 quart
CREAM, hot	2 cups
SHERRY	½ cup
TOAST	25 slices

Procedure

1. Combine seafood.
2. Melt butter; blend in flour and seasonings.
3. Gradually add hot milk and cream; cook and stir until thickened and smooth.
4. Add sherry and seafood. Heat through.
5. Serve on toast points.

Procedure

1. If scallops are frozen, defrost. Rinse and dry.
2. Melt butter. Add onion; saute until tender but not browned.
3. Remove from heat; blend in flour. Gradually add hot milk. Cook and stir over medium heat until sauce is smooth and thickened.
4. Add salt and cayenne. Cover; cook over low heat 10 minutes. Stir in tomato paste, cream and sherry.
5. Add scallops; cook 8 to 10 minutes. Serve on rice, toast points or in patty shells.

CRAB CAKES

Serve with French fries and a mixed green salad with ripe tomato wedges.

Yield: 45 portions

Ingredients

DEHYDRATED ONION	3 tablespoons
CRABMEAT, flaked	7 pounds
WORCESTERSHIRE SAUCE	2 tablespoons
LEMON JUICE from	2 lemons
CAYENNE PEPPER	½ teaspoon
BUTTER or MARGARINE	½ pound
FLOUR, all purpose, sifted	1 cup
SALT	2 tablespoons
MILK	1½ quarts
EGGS, beaten	10
GROUND NUTMEG	1 teaspoon
BREAD CRUMBS, fine white	1 quart
MAYONNAISE	1½ quarts
CUCUMBERS, chopped and well drained	2 cups

Procedure

1. Reconstitute the onion. Mix with crab, Worcestershire, lemon juice and cayenne pepper.

2. Melt butter; blend in flour and salt. Add milk gradually. Cook and stir over low heat until thickened. Cool.

3. Beat half of the eggs into the cream sauce. Add nutmeg. Combine with crabmeat mixture.

4. Place in a shallow pan; chill until stiff.

5. Shape into flat cakes. Dip in remaining beaten eggs; roll in bread crumbs.

6. Fry in deep fat at 370°F. until well browned.

7. Combine mayonnaise and cucumbers. Serve as a sauce with the crab cakes.

SHRIMP DEWEY

Present with a salad of peach halves stuffed with chopped prunes and walnuts. And offer molasses drop cookies by way of dessert.

Yield: 48 portions

Ingredients

SHRIMP, raw, in shell (16 to 20 count)	12 pounds
COURT BOUILLON, boiling	as needed
BUTTER or MARGARINE	8 ounces
CREAM SAUCE, rich	1¼ gallons
CREAM, light	2 cups
SWEET PEPPER FLAKES	½ cup
MUSTARD, dry	3 tablespoons
INSTANT ONION POWDER	2 tablespoons
SALT	2 tablespoons
WHITE PEPPER, ground	1 teaspoon
MUSHROOMS, sliced, cooked	2 quarts
CAYENNE	½ teaspoon
DUCHESS POTATOES	as needed
PAPRIKA	as needed

Procedure

1. Add shrimp to boiling court bouillon to cover. Return to boiling; cook 4 to 5 minutes. Cool. Peel; devein. Cut shrimp into pieces.

2. Melt butter; saute shrimp lightly, 2 to 3 minutes. Do not brown.

3. Combine cream sauce, cream and seasonings; blend well. Heat to boiling point, stirring constantly.

4. Add shrimp, mushrooms and cayenne. Simmer gently 5 minutes.

5. Pipe a border of Duchess potatoes around edge of individual serving dishes. Brown lightly under broiler.

6. Ladle shrimp mixture into center of potatoes. Sprinkle with paprika.

SAVORY SALMON PIE

A leafy green salad with slices of raw mushrooms makes a sprightly companion for this good looking casserole. Squares of yellow sheet cake with baked-on praline topping suggests a likely dessert to round out the meal.

Yield: 24 portions

Ingredients

SALMON, canned	6 pounds
GREEN BEANS, diagonal-cut; drained	1 No. 10 can
SWEET PICKLE RELISH, drained	¾ cup
BUTTER	½ pound
FLOUR	5 ounces
MILK	1½ quarts
SALT	2½ teaspoons
PEPPER	¾ teaspoon
CHEESE, process American, sharp	12 ounces
POTATOES, instant mashed	as needed
SOUR CREAM	1½ cups
CHIVES, frozen	4 teaspoons
BUTTER, melted	as needed

Procedure

1. Drain salmon; remove bones; flake.
2. Combine salmon, beans and pickle relish.
3. Melt butter; blend in flour. Gradually add milk. Cook and stir until blended and thickened.
4. Add seasonings and cheese; stir until cheese melts. Combine with salmon mixture.
5. Prepare sufficient instant mashed potatoes to yield 2 quarts, using package directions, reducing total liquid by 1½ cups.
6. Add sour cream and chives. Turn salmon mixture into 24 individual casseroles. Top with a No. 12 scoop of seasoned potato topping. Or, pipe potato rosettes on top, using pastry bag.
8. Brush potato with melted butter.
9. Bake in a 375°F. oven 20 to 25 minutes or until potatoes are lightly browned.

SHRIMP CREOLE

To provide an appealing contrast for this dish serve with green peas and a small Caesar salad.

Yield: 32 portions

Ingredients

ONION, thinly sliced	1 pound, 8 ounces
CELERY, cut in ¼-inch crescents	1 pound, 2 ounces
GREEN PEPPER, chopped	12 ounces
GARLIC, minced	½ teaspoon
MARGARINE	5 ounces
FLOUR	3 ounces
TOMATOES, canned	1 gallon
SHRIMP, raw, cleaned	3 pounds, 6 ounces
or	
SHRIMP, cooked	2 pounds, 2 ounces
OKRA, canned, drained	2 pounds, 2 ounces
BAY LEAVES	2
SALT	¾ ounce
SUGAR	1 ounce
WORCESTERSHIRE SAUCE	2 tablespoons
RICE, cooked, hot	1¼ gallons

Procedure

1. Saute onion, celery, green pepper and garlic in margarine. Add flour; mix well.
2. Dip tomatoes out of can. Strain juice to remove seeds.
3. When using raw shrimp, add to tomatoes; simmer until done, 4 to 7 minutes. When using cooked shrimp, just add with tomatoes to vegetables.
4. Combine sauteed vegetables, tomatoes and shrimp, okra and seasonings. Heat thoroughly but do not boil.
5. Serve over rice.

Variation: For Seafood Creole, reduce amount of cooked shrimp to 1 pound. Add 1 pound, 2 ounces of cooked, flaked fish (all breading, bones and hard crust removed).

ROLLED FLOUNDER WITH GREEN GODDESS DRESSING

An exciting new presentation for chilled poached fish. A popular choice with a cup of hot consomme, whole wheat rolls and streusel-topped red cherry pie.

Yield: 12 portions (3 rolls each)

Ingredients

FLOUNDER FILLETS	18
SEASONED SALT	as needed
SEASONED PEPPER	as needed
PARSLEY, chopped	1½ cups
WATER or COURT BOUILLON	as needed
GREEN GODDESS DRESSING*	1 quart

Procedure

1. Sprinkle fillets with seasoned salt, seasoned pepper and chopped parsley. Roll up, beginning at thicker end. Fasten with wooden pick.

2. Simmer in water or court bouillon until just done, about 10 minutes. Remove from liquid; refrigerate.

3. Cut chilled rolls crosswise into two pieces. Arrange on crisp greens, allowing three rolls per portion. Serve with green goddess dressing.

*GREEN GODDESS DRESSING
Yield: 1 quart

Ingredients

ANCHOVY FILLETS	8 to 10
GREEN ONION	1
CHIVES, finely cut	1/4 cup
PARSLEY, finely chopped	1/3 cup
TARRAGON, fresh, finely cut**	2 tablespoons
MAYONNAISE	3 cups
VINEGAR, tarragon	1/4 cup
GARLIC, crushed	1 small clove

Procedure

1. Chop anchovies and green onion together until very finely cut. Add chives, parsley and fresh tarragon.

2. Combine mayonnaise, vinegar and juice from garlic. Add anchovy mixture; mix lightly but well.

**Or 1 tablespoon dried tarragon. Soak in the tarragon vinegar; strain vinegar.

SALMON CREPES BAYOU

Tender, thin pancakes with a tasty filling and sauce—a distinguished entree to present with a tossed green salad and fruit dessert.

Yield: 12 portions

Ingredients

CREPES
FLOUR, sifted	¾ cup (3 ounces)
SALT	¼ teaspoon
EGGS, beaten	2
MILK	1 cup

FILLING AND SAUCE
ONION, chopped	1 teaspoon
BUTTER or MARGARINE	3 tablespoons
FLOUR	¼ cup
SALT	¼ teaspoon
PEPPER, white	dash
NUTMEG	dash
MILK and CREAM	1½ cups
EGG YOLKS, beaten	2
PARMESAN CHEESE	2 tablespoons
SHERRY	2 tablespoons
SALMON, drained, flaked	1 1-pound can

Procedure

To make crepes: 1. Sift flour and salt together.

2. Combine egg and milk. Add to flour mixture; stir until batter is smooth.

3. Drop 2 tablespoons of batter into a hot buttered crepe pan. Cook until browned on underside; turn to brown other side.

To prepare filling and sauce: 1. Saute onion in butter until tender. Blend in flour and seasonings.

2. Add milk gradually; stir and cook until thickened.

3. Add a little hot sauce to egg yolks; blend. Add to remaining sauce, stirring constantly.

4. Add cheese and sherry; blend.

5. Combine ½ cup of the sauce with the salmon. Reserve remaining sauce to serve on crepes.

6. Spread about 2 tablespoons of filling on each crepe. Roll like a jelly roll. Place on baking sheet. Heat in a 350°F. oven 10 to 15 minutes.

7. Heat reserved sauce, thinning with a little cream, if desired. Spoon sauce over each crepe just before serving.

CODFISH BALLS

An old-fashioned dish with a modern touch!

Yield: 50 portions (2 2-ounce balls)

Ingredients

SALT CODFISH, boneless	5 pounds
WATER, boiling	2½ quarts
INSTANT MASHED POTATOES	2 pounds (1 quart)
MILK, hot	3 cups
EGGS, unbeaten	1 pound (2 cups)
PEPPER	½ teaspoon
ONION, finely chopped	¾ cup
PARSLEY, finely chopped	½ cup
LEMON JUICE	½ cup

Procedure

1. Freshen and cook codfish according to package directions. Cool; flake. (Amount of flaked fish should be about 4 pounds or 1 gallon.)

2. Pour boiling water into mixer bowl. Gradually add potatoes, whipping at medium speed until well blended (about 1 minute).

3. Add milk gradually, then eggs, whipping until light and fluffy. Mix in pepper, onion, parsley, lemon juice and codfish. Season with salt, if desired.

4. Shape into balls, using No. 20 scoop. If desired, roll in flour or other coating mixtures. Fry in deep fat at 375°F. about 3 minutes or until golden brown. Or, if desired, shape mixture into patties; brown on both sides on greased grill or in skillet.

5. Serve hot with tomato or egg sauce.

SHRIMP CURRY

Accompaniments for this curry might include chopped parsley, chopped cashews, coconut, popadams and chutney. For dessert: lemon sherbet with a light splash of brandy.

Yield: 50 4-ounce portions

Ingredients

SHRIMP, raw, shelled, deveined	7½ pounds
SHORTENING	4 ounces
WATER	1 gallon
CURRY POWDER	3 tablespoons
CLOVES, whole (tied in cheesecloth)	6
SALT	5 tablespoons
PEPPER, black	1 teaspoon
MONOSODIUM GLUTAMATE	1½ teaspoon
LEMON RIND, grated from	2 lemons
LEMON JUICE, from	2 lemons
BUTTER or MARGARINE	2 ounces
ONIONS, diced	8 ounces
APPLES, tart, diced	1½ pounds
BUTTER or MARGARINE	4 ounces
FLOUR	1¼ cups
WATER	1 quart
RAISINS, seedless	1 pound
RICE, cooked	1½ gallons

Procedure

1. Cut shrimp in halves lengthwise. Saute lightly in shortening. Drain off fat.

2. Bring first amount of water to boil. Add spices, seasonings, lemon rind and juice. Reduce to simmer.

3. Saute onions and apples in first amount of butter; add to water and seasonings.

4. Blend remaining butter with flour; add second amount of water gradually, stirring to keep mixture smooth. Add to spice mixture.

5. Add raisins; simmer until plump. Add shrimp; continue simmering just until shrimp are done.

6. Serve over rice.

Apple Braised Shortribs (recipe p. 172)

Processed Apples Institute

MEAT

"MORE STYLE THAN MONEY" sounds the keynote for the recipes that make up the section devoted to meats. This assortment, which takes into account dishes made with beef, fresh and cured pork, lamb and veal, places its emphasis on the less expensive items fashioned with a difference.

As a modest sampling:

An unusual meat and vegetable combination puts ground beef and pork with slices of eggplant, tomato and onion.

Gingersnap crumbs and plump dark raisins distinguish the sauce for a meat ball creation.

A well-spiced version of curried lamb boasts an inspired accent of tart, juicy grapes.

Sweetbreads and chipped beef combine their forces for an original concoction to present in a popover and garnish with almonds.

Roast beef hash becomes ultra special when it appears in a pastry shell topped with an eye-catching "pinwheel" of pimiento and cheese.

But, there's really no end to the good things that can happen when imagination deals with economy and holds the upper hand!

APPLE BRAISED SHORTRIBS
(Picture on page 171.)

A savory dish that combines well with noodles or whipped potatoes, a shredded lettuce salad and ice cream pie in a walnut crust.

Yield: 25 portions

Ingredients

FLOUR	1 cup
SALT	2 tablespoons
PEPPER	1 tablespoon
SHORTRIBS OF BEEF	25 pounds
APPLE SLICES	1 No. 10 can
CORNSTARCH	4 tablespoons
VINEGAR, cider	1 cup
SUGAR, light brown	12 ounces (2 cups packed)
TOMATO PASTE	1 cup
GINGER, ground	2 tablespoons

Procedure

1. Combine flour, salt and pepper. Dredge shortribs thoroughly.
2. Place meat in a 12-inch by 20-inch by 4-inch baking pan. Bake in a 350°F. oven one hour, turning meat occasionally, to brown on all sides.
3. Drain excess fat from pan; continue baking for one hour.
4. Drain apples. Combine juice from apples and cornstarch. Stir until smooth. Add vinegar, brown sugar, tomato paste and ginger. Bring to a boil; cook until slightly thickened and smooth.
5. Add apple slices. Pour mixture over meat; continue baking for another hour. (Total baking time, 3 hours).

CREAMED CHIPPED BEEF AND EGGS EN CASSEROLE

Serve with an orange Waldorf salad and offer a chocolate layer cake with mocha icing for dessert.

Yield: 25 portions

Ingredients

CHIPPED BEEF	2 pounds
CREAM	2 cups
CREAM SAUCE	3 quarts
BUTTER	¼ pound
EGGS, hard-cooked, quartered	12
SALT	1 tablespoon
PEPPER	1 teaspoon
WORCESTERSHIRE SAUCE	2 tablespoons
PARSLEY, chopped	½ cup

HAM 'N ASPARAGUS CASSEROLE

Try starting the menu with a wedge of melon and ending it with Gingerbread squares topped with orange sauce.

Yield: 24 portions

Ingredients

EGG NOODLES, cooked	3 quarts
HAM, cooked, diced	3 pounds
SOUR CREAM	1½ quarts
CREAM, light	2¼ cups
FLOUR, all-purpose	½ cup
SALT	1 tablespoon
PEPPER	¼ teaspoon
CUT ASPARAGUS SPEARS, drained	½ No. 10 can
BUTTER or MARGARINE, melted	2 ounces
PARMESAN CHEESE, grated	¾ cup

Procedure

1. Combine noodles and ham.

2. Blend sour cream with light cream, flour and seasonings. Pour over noodle mixture; mix thoroughly. Turn into greased 12-inch by 20-inch baking pan.

3. Layer drained asparagus on top of noodle mixture. Drizzle with butter. Sprinkle with cheese.

4. Bake in a 350°F. oven 30 to 35 minutes.

Procedure

1. Boil chipped beef 2 to 3 minutes. Drain; combine with cream and cream sauce. Simmer 5 minutes or until sauce is of desired consistency.

2. Blend in butter. Add eggs.

3. Remove from heat; add seasonings and parsley.

4. Serve in casserole with toast points.

WESTERN WEINERS

Fordhook limas, sliced tomatoes and rice custard pudding with dates can form a good menu relationship with this easy-to-fix dish.

Yield: 50 portions

Ingredients

ONIONS, finely chopped	1 quart
CELERY, chopped	1 quart
GARLIC, minced	1 clove
SHORTENING	10 ounces (1½ cups)
ALL PURPOSE BARBECUE SAUCE (prepared)	2 quarts
WATER	1 quart
FRANKFURTERS, scored	100 (12 pounds)

Procedure

1. Brown onions, celery and garlic in shortening.
2. Add barbecue sauce and water, stirring well. Add frankfurters. Cover; simmer 10 minutes.

DELUXE CREAMED CHIPPED BEEF

Bill with a tomato and sliced egg salad and offer frozen pineapple chunks and ginger cookies for dessert.

Yield: 20 portions

Ingredients

CHIPPED BEEF	1 pound
BUTTER	½ pound
ONION, finely chopped	½ cup
FLOUR	1 cup
MILK	1½ quarts
MUSHROOM PIECES	2 8-ounce cans
CHEESE, shredded	1 pound
PARSLEY, chopped	½ cup
SOUR CREAM	2 cups
SALT	as needed
PEPPER, white	as needed

Procedure

1. Cut beef in strips.
2. Melt butter; add beef and onion; saute until onion is transparent and beef is frizzled.
3. Blend in flour. Add milk gradually, stirring until sauce is thickened.
4. Add mushroom pieces, cheese and parsley; stir until cheese melts.
5. Add sour cream. Season with salt and pepper.
6. Serve over toasted English muffins, spoonbread, baked potato or buttered toast triangles.

SWEDISH MEAT LOAF WITH ONION SAUCE
Baked potatoes and hot pickled beets complete a hearty plate.

Yield: 48 portions, 6 8½-inch by 4½-inch by 2½-inch pans.

Ingredients

GROUND BEEF	6 pounds
GROUND VEAL	4 pounds
ROLLED OATS (quick or old-fashioned), uncooked	1 quart
EGGS	6
MILK	1 quart
SALT	2 tablespoons
PEPPER	1 teaspoon
NUTMEG	1½ teaspoons

Procedure

1. Combine ground meats, oats, eggs, milk and seasonings, mixing lightly but thoroughly. (On mixer beat at low speed about 2 minutes.)

2. Pack 2½ pounds mixture into each of six 8½-inch by 4½-inch by 2½-inch loaf pans. Bake in a 375°F. oven 1 to 1¼ hours.

3. Let stand 5 minutes before slicing. Cut each loaf into 8 slices. Serve hot with onion sauce.

ONION SAUCE
Yield: 1¾ quarts

Ingredients

ONION, chopped	2 cups
BUTTER or MARGARINE	½ cup
FLOUR	½ cup
CARAWAY SEED (optional)	1 tablespoon
SALT	1½ teaspoons
WHITE PEPPER	½ teaspoon
MILK	1½ quarts

Procedure

1. Cook onion in butter until tender.

2. Blend in flour and seasonings. Add milk gradually stirring constantly.

3. Cook over medium heat 15 to 20 minutes, stirring frequently, until smooth and thick.

CREAMY PORK HASH

A welcome answer for leftover roast pork. Serve with a shredded carrot, raisin and peanut salad and top off the meal with a glazed open-face red cherry tart.

Yield: 24 portions

Ingredients

ONIONS, sliced	1 pound
BUTTER or MARGARINE	9 ounces
CREAM OF MUSHROOM SOUP	1 50-ounce can
MILK	3 cups
WORCESTERSHIRE SAUCE	2 tablespoons
INSTANT GRANULATED GARLIC	½ to 1 teaspoon
LIQUID HOT PEPPER SEASONING	few drops
PORK, cooked, diced	3 pounds
POTATOES, cooked, diced	3 pounds
PEAS, cooked	1½ pounds
PAPRIKA	2 tablespoons

Procedure

1. Saute onions in butter until tender.
2. Blend in soup, milk, Worcestershire, garlic and pepper seasoning.
3. Add remaining ingredients. Cook over low heat 10 minutes or until heated through, stirring frequently.

SAVORY OLIVE FRANKFURTER RAMEKINS

Try billing with a molded vegetable salad, bran muffins and a fresh fruit dessert.

Yield: 15 portions

Ingredients

RIPE OLIVES, pitted	1½ cups
CHEESE, CHEDDAR, shredded	12 ounces
HORSERADISH, prepared	3 tablespoons
MAYONNAISE	3 tablespoons
FRANKFURTERS	30
TOMATO SAUCE	3 cups
POTATOES, mashed, hot	1½ quarts
BUTTER, melted	as needed

GARDEN COURT LAMB SHOULDER CHOPS

As a menu suggestion, combine with an apricot salad and chocolate brownies.

Yield: 48 portions

Ingredients

LAMB SHOULDER CHOPS, ½-inch thick	48
FLOUR	as needed
SHORTENING	as needed
SALT	¼ cup
PEPPER	1 teaspoon
POTATOES, quartered	6 pounds
CARROTS, quartered lengthwise	6 pounds
WHITE TURNIPS, julienne	4 pounds
ONION, chopped	3 pounds
WATER	1½ to 2 quarts
PARSLEY, chopped	as needed

Procedure

1. Dredge lamb in flour. Brown in a small amount of shortening. Sprinkle with salt and pepper.

2. Place meat in baking pans; arrange vegetables over and around meat.

3. Add water; cover. Bake in a 325°F. oven 35 to 45 minutes or until meat and vegetables are done. Add water during cooking, if necessary.

4. Sprinkle generously with chopped parsley before serving.

Procedure

1. Cut olives in wedges. Combine with cheese, horseradish and mayonnaise.

2. Slit frankfurters lengthwise, cutting almost all the way through. Fill each with about 1 tablespoon olive mixture.

3. For each portion, place 2 frankfurters in a ramekin; cover with tomato sauce.

4. Bake in a 400°F. oven 15 to 20 minutes. Pipe or spoon potatoes on either side of frankfurters. Brush lightly with butter. Run under broiler 5 minutes or until browned.

QUINCY HOUSE SWISS STEAK

Mashed potatoes are a natural with this dish.

Yield: 90 6-ounce portions (cooked weight)

Ingredients

PEPPERS, green, chopped	10 pounds
MUSHROOMS, sliced	3 pounds
ONIONS, chopped	2 pounds
TOMATOES, canned	2 No. 10 cans
HOT PEPPER SAUCE	½ teaspoon
SALT AND PEPPER	as needed
WATER or STOCK	3 gallons
BEEF, bottom round	45 pounds
FLOUR	1 pound
SALT	1½ tablespoons

Procedure

1. Combine the vegetables, seasonings and water; cook in steam jacketed kettle to blend the flavors.

2. Cut bottom round into ½-inch slices and into portions weighing approximately 8 ounces. Score with a sharp knife to sever fibers so steak will not curl when broiled.

3. Dredge steaks in seasoned flour; brown under broiler.

4. Overlap steaks in roasting pans; cover with sauce. Cover pans; cook in a 300°F. oven for 2½ to 3 hours or until tender.

Note: Steaks may be returned to steam jacketed kettle with sauce and held for service; do not allow to dry out on top of range or in oven.

HAMBURGER STROGANOFF

Serve with buttered cauliflower and/or a pickled beet and onion salad.

Yield: 50 portions

Ingredients

INSTANT CHOPPED ONION	2 cups
GROUND BEEF	8 pounds
MUSHROOMS, sliced	2 pounds
SHORTENING	¾ cup
FLOUR	½ cup
CREAM OF MUSHROOM SOUP	3 50-ounce cans
SALT	1 tablespoon
INSTANT GRANULATED GARLIC	1 teaspoon
SOUR CREAM	1½ quarts
NOODLES	3 pounds
BUTTER or MARGARINE	¼ pound
POPPY SEEDS	¼ cup

Procedure

1. Rehydrate onions.
2. Saute ground beef, mushrooms and onions in shortening until beef is browned and vegetables are tender.
3. Stir in flour; blend well.
4. Blend in soup, salt and garlic. Simmer 15 to 20 minutes. Stir in sour cream; heat through.
5. Cook noodles; drain. Toss hot noodles with butter and poppy seed.
6. To serve, put about 2/3 cup noodles in heated casserole. Top with about 2/3 cup meat mixture.

CORNBREAD AND SAUSAGE

Serve with halves of cantaloupe or broiled grapefruit. Or, begin the meal with chilled fruit juice and serve apricots on scalloped apples or the plate beside the cornbread square.

Yield: 16 portions

Ingredients

EGGS	5
WATER	3 cups
CORNBREAD MIX	2½ pounds
SAUSAGE, brown and serve	32 links

Procedure

1. Blend eggs and water in mixing bowl.
2. Add cornbread mix; blend until smooth. Do not overmix.
3. Divide batter into two jelly roll pans, 15½-inches by 10½-inches. Arrange 16 sausage links in the batter in each pan.
4. Bake in a 425°F. oven 15 minutes or until done.
5. Cut 8 portions per pan. Serve with syrup, if desired.

SOUTHERN HAM SHORTCAKE

Combines well with buttered broccoli spears and a fresh fruit dessert.

Yield: 48 portions

Ingredients

HAM, fully cooked	6 pounds
BUTTER or MARGARINE	¾ pound
FLOUR	2 cups
MILK, hot	1 gallon
CHEESE, sharp process Cheddar, grated	1½ pounds
MUSHROOMS, pieces and stems	3 cups
SALT	2 teaspoons
PEPPER	1 teaspoon
GREEN PEPPER, minced	¾ cup
YELLOW CORNBREAD	48 squares

Procedure

1. Cut ham in julienne strips about 1 inch long.
2. Melt butter. Add flour; blend
3. Add hot milk and grated cheese. Cook over medium heat, stirring constantly, until sauce is thick and smooth.
4. Add ham, mushrooms, seasonings and green pepper.
5. Serve hot over split squares of cornbread.

Cornbread and Sausage

Pillsbury Food Service Div.

MEATBALLS IN GINGERSNAP SAUCE

Hash brown potatoes go well with these meatballs with their spicy sauce.
So do chilled canned pears, as a salad or dessert.

Yield: 24 portions

Ingredients

GROUND BEEF	5 pounds
EGGS, beaten	5
BREAD CRUMBS, soft	1 quart
WATER	1¼ cups
INSTANT MICHED ONION	¼ cup
SALT	2½ teaspoons
INSTANT GRANULATED GARLIC	¾ teaspoon
PEPPER	½ teaspoon
BEEF STOCK	7½ cups
SUGAR, brown	9 ounces
RAISINS, dark seedless	1¼ cups
LEMON JUICE	¾ cup
GINGERSNAPS, crushed to coarse crumbs	2½ cups

Procedure

1. Combine meat, eggs, bread crumbs, water, onion, salt, garlic and pepper. Shape into balls, using No. 16 scoop.

2. Combine stock, brown sugar, raisins, lemon juice and gingersnap crumbs; bring to boiling.

3. Add meat balls. Cook, uncovered, over low heat 10 minutes.

4. Turn meatballs, spooning sauce over them. Cook 10 minutes longer, stirring occasionally.

CREAMED SWEETBREADS WITH CHIPPED BEEF AND ALMONDS

Present with buttered green peas, a Chinese cabbage salad and wedges of watermelon for dessert.

Yield: 50 portions

Ingredients

SWEETBREADS	25 pairs
WATER, cold	as needed
SALT	as needed
VINEGAR	as needed
CHIPPED BEEF	3 pounds
MUSHROOMS, sliced	1 gallon
BUTTER or MARGARINE	1½ pounds
FLOUR	3 cups
MILK	2 gallons
ALMONDS, slivered, toasted	1 pound

Procedure

1. Cover sweetbreads with cold water; soak for ½ hour. Add salt and vinegar allowing 2 teaspoons salt and ¼ cup vinegar for each 3 quarts water.

2. Parboil for 20 minutes. Drain. Remove loose membranes; slice.

3. Saute sweetbreads, chipped beef and mushrooms in butter 3 to 4 minutes.

4. Blend in flour. Add milk slowly stirring until sauce thickens.

5. Serve on toast or hot buttered rice or in hot popover shells. Garnish with almonds.

CORNED BEEF HASH WITH PEACHES

Toasted English muffins team well with this fruit topped hash. A creamy vanilla pudding garnished with topping and chopped nuts provides a welcome dessert.

Yield: 27 portions

Ingredients

CORNED BEEF HASH	2 No. 10 cans
CLING PEACH HALVES, drained	27
SWEET PICKLE RELISH	1½ cups
PREPARED MUSTARD	6 tablespoons

Procedure

1. Portion corned beef hash into individual baking dishes, allowing 8 ounces (1 cup) per portion. Make a slight indentation in center. Place peach half, cut side up, in center of hash.

2. Combine pickle relish and mustard. Spoon about 1 tablespoon mixture into each peach half.

3. Place baking dishes on sheet pans. Bake in a 350°F. oven 20 min.

Variations

For *SUGAR 'N CREAM-GLAZED PEACHES AND HASH,* omit pickle relish mixture. Blend 1/3 cup peach syrup, 2/3 cup light cream, 1/3 cup prepared mustard and 1/3 cup brown sugar. Spoon over peaches; bake as above.

For *TANGY MUSTARD-GLAZED PEACHES AND HASH,* omit pickle relish mixture. Blend 2/3 cup brown sugar, 2 tablespoons dry mustard, 1/3 cup lemon juice and ½ teaspoon salt. Spoon over peaches; bake as above.

CURRIED LAMB WITH GRAPES
Garnish the curry with coconut and, for an extra flourish, present with chutney.

Yield: 48 portions

Ingredients

LAMB SHOULDER, boneless	16 pounds
SALAD OIL or SHORTENING	as needed
FLOUR	1 cup
CURRY POWDER	1/2 cup
STOCK or WATER	3 quarts
INSTANT MINCED ONION	1 cup
SALT	1/3 cup
GINGER, ground	2 teaspoons
MUSTARD, powdered	2 teaspoons
CARDAMON, ground	2 teaspoons
INSTANT GARLIC POWDER	3/4 teaspoon
EVAPORATED MILK	2 cups
SEEDLESS GRAPES	3 quarts

Procedure

1. Trim any excess fat from lamb. Cut meat into 1-inch cubes.
2. Brown meat in oil, turning to brown all sides.
3. Stir in flour and curry powder; cook and stir 2 minutes.
4. Add stock and seasonings. Cover; simmer 1 to 1¼ hours or until lamb is tender.
5. Stir in evaporated milk and grapes. Bring just to boiling point. Serve over hot cooked rice, if desired.

STEAK STRIPS WITH SOYA SAUCE

Try serving with a Caesar salad and with banana cream pie for dessert.

Yield: 24 portions

Ingredients

ROUND STEAK, ½-inch thick	8 pounds
BUTTER or MARGARINE	¾ pound
SOYA SAUCE	1½ cups
WATER	as needed
CELERY, sliced diagonally	1 gallon
CORNSTARCH	¾ cup
WATER	1½ cups
RICE, cooked	4½ quarts

Procedure

1. Cut steak into strips ½-inch wide and 2-inches long.
2. Brown steak strips in butter, very quickly.
3. Combine soya sauce with enough water to make 2 quarts; add to meat. Add celery.
4. Simmer, covered, until meat and celery are tender.
5. Blend cornstarch with water; thicken the meat mixture, stirring until clear.
6. Serve over hot fluffy rice.

VEGETABLE BEEF LOAF

Creamed shredded green cabbage complements this unusual meat loaf. An old-fashioned strawberry shortcake makes a congenial dessert.

Yield: 4 loaves 9-inch by 5-inch by 3-inch.

Ingredients

ONIONS, peeled	6 ounces
GREEN PEPPERS, seeded	8 ounces
POTATOES, peeled	1½ pounds
CARROTS, peeled	1 pound
BEEF, ground	6 pounds
TOMATO JUICE	4½ cups
EGGS	6
SALT	2½ tablespoons
PEPPER	1½ teaspoons
BREAD CRUMBS, fine dry	1¼ quarts

CURRIED GREEN BEANS AND VEAL

Try accompanying with a green and red pepper relish, and offer a frozen fruit salad by way of dessert.

Yield: 50 portions

Ingredients

GREEN BEANS, French style	2 No. 10 cans
COOKED VEAL, cubed	3½ pounds
BUTTER or MARGARINE	½ pound
CURRY POWDER	2 tablespoons
ONION, finely chopped	½ cup
FLOUR	1 cup
SALT	1 tablespoon
PEPPER	½ teaspoon
MILK	2 quarts
RICE, cooked, hot	2 gallons

Procedure

1. Drain green beans; combine with veal.
2. Melt butter; add curry powder; add onion. Cook until onion is crisply tender.
3. Blend in flour, salt and pepper. Stir in milk, gradually. Cook and stir until mixture is thickened.
4. Add beans and veal. Heat thoroughly.
5. Serve on mounds of hot cooked rice.

▼   ▼

Procedure

1. Grind raw vegetables together.
2. Combine with remaining ingredients; mix well.
3. Line ends and bottoms of four 9-inch by 5-inch by 3-inch loaf pans with strips of brown paper; grease well.
4. Pack meat mixture in pans. Bake in a 325°F. oven 1½ hours or until meat is well done.
5. Let cool 10 minutes before removing from pans. Turn out; slice into portions.

CORNED BEEF AND CABBAGE ROLLS

The popular corned beef and cabbage team combines talents again to create a delightful new version of a famous old dish.

Yield: 48 portions

Ingredients

CABBAGE	20 pounds
ONIONS, chopped	1½ quarts
GREEN PEPPERS, chopped	6 large
SHORTENING	½ cup
MUSTARD, powdered	2 tablespoons
WATER, warm	2 to 3 tablespoons
POTATOES, cooked, diced	10 pounds
CORNED BEEF, cooked, chopped	10 pounds
SALT	2 tablespoons
BLACK PEPPER, ground	4 teaspoons
EGGS	6
HERBED TOMATO SAUCE (facing page)	2 quarts

Procedure

1. Core cabbage. Parboil in boiling salted water 10 minutes or until leaves are tender. Drain. Separate leaves.

2. Saute onions and green peppers in shortening until tender but not brown.

3. Blend mustard with warm water; let stand 10 minutes to develop flavor.

4. Combine potatoes, corned beef, sauteed vegetable mixture, salt, pepper, mustard and eggs; mix thoroughly.

5. Place about ¼ cup of the hash in a cabbage leaf. Fold in the ends; roll tightly. Place in greased baking pans, seam side down.

6. Cover with the herbed tomato sauce. Bake in a 375°F. oven 45 to 50 minutes, basting occasionally.

7. Serve hot with additional herbed tomato sauce.

American Dairy Association

HERBED TOMATO SAUCE
Yield: 48 portions

Ingredients

ONIONS, chopped	1 quart
GARLIC, minced	2 cloves
COOKING OIL or SHORTENING	1 cup
FLOUR	1½ cups
STOCK	3 quarts
SALT	2 tablespoons
BLACK PEPPER, ground	1 teaspoon
THYME LEAVES	1 teaspoon
BAY LEAVES	2
WHOLE CLOVES	4
BASIL LEAVES	2 tablespoons
SUGAR	2 tablespoons
TOMATOES, fresh, peeled, chopped	10 pounds

Procedure

1. Saute onion and garlic in oil until tender but not brown.
2. Blend in flour. Gradually stir in stock. Bring to a boil; cook and stir until smooth.
3. Add remaining ingredients. Simmer for one to 1½ hours.
4. Correct seasoning, if necessary. Strain through a fine china cap.

BAKED ITALIAN MEAT LOAF

Try offering with chopped spinach or broccoli and a crusty whole-grain bread with lemon ice or spumoni on the dessert agenda.

Yield: 48 portions

Ingredients

BREAD CRUMBS, dry	1 quart
WATER	1½ quarts
BEEF, ground, raw	8 pounds
PARSLEY, chopped	2 tablespoons
ONION, chopped	2 cups
CHEESE PARMESAN	1 cup
EGGS	8
SALT	2½ tablespoons
PEPPER	1 teaspoon
TOMATO SAUCE	1 quart
CHEESE, mozzarella, shredded	½ pound
OREGANO	2 tablespoons

Procedure

1. Combine crumbs and water; mix.

2. Add ground beef, parsley, onion, Parmesan cheese, eggs, salt and pepper; mix well.

3. Turn into a large steam table pan. Bake in a 375°F. oven for 50 minutes.

4. Spread tomato sauce, mozzarella cheese and oregano over surface of meat. Continue baking for 30 minutes more.

FRANKFURTER MEAL-IN-ONE

To complete the menu, add individual tomato aspic rings filled with cole slaw and Dutch apple pie.

Yield: 50 portions

Ingredients

INSTANT SLICED POTATOES	1 2¼-pound package
GREEN BEANS, cut, canned, undrained	1½ quarts
MILK and LIQUID FROM BEANS	3 quarts
BUTTER or MARGARINE	½ pound
ONIONS, chopped	1 quart
GREEN PEPPERS, chopped	1 cup
FLOUR	2 cups (8 ounces)
SALT	2 teaspoons
FRANKFURTERS, cut in thirds	5¼ pounds
CHEESE, sharp cheddar, grated	1 pound

Procedure

1. Cook potatoes according to package directions.

2. Drain beans; measure liquid. Add milk to make required amount.

3. Melt butter in heavy saucepan; add onions and peppers; cook until tender, about 5 minutes.

4. Blend in flour and salt. Gradually add liquid, stirring constantly until thickened. Carefully stir in potatoes and beans.

5. Arrange layers of vegetable mixture and frankfurters in two 20-inch by 12-inch by 2-inch pans, ending with frankfurters on top.

6. Sprinkle with cheese. Bake in a 350°F. oven about 30 minutes or until thoroughly heated through.

PORCUPINE MEAT BALLS

Try mashed winter squash or rutabagas as a go-along.

Yield: 24 portions

Ingredients

ONIONS, finely chopped	1½ cups
VINEGAR	¼ cup
WORCESTERSHIRE SAUCE	¼ cup
CHILI POWDER	2 teaspoons
CATSUP	1½ cups
WATER	2½ cups
SALT	2 teaspoons
GROUND BEEF	3 pounds
PORK, lean, ground	1 pound
GARLIC, minced (optional)	1 clove
PEPPER	1 teaspoon
EGGS	3
MILK	¾ cup
RICE, uncooked	1 cup
SALT	2 tablespoons

Procedure

1. Combine onions, vinegar, Worcestershire, chili powder, catsup, water and salt in a 25-inch by 15-inch by 2-inch baking pan. Bring to a boil.

2. Combine ground beef, pork, garlic, pepper, eggs, milk, raw rice and salt; mix well.

3. Shape meat mixture into 48 balls (about 1½ inches in diameter). Drop the balls into the boiling sauce.

4. Roll balls over to coat with sauce.

5. Cover pan with foil. Bake in a 350°F. oven 50 minutes.

VEAL AND MUSHROOM CASSEROLE

Try teaming with a salad of red ripe tomatoes. And for dessert, offer orange sherbet topped with shaved sweet chocolate.

Yield: 48 portions—¾ cup veal, ½ cup noodles, 1 tablespoon almonds

Ingredients

SALT	1 ounce
PEPPER	1 teaspoon
VEAL, lean shoulder, cut in 2-inch pieces	16 pounds
ONIONS, chopped	1 quart
BUTTER or MARGARINE	1 pound
WATER, hot	1 gallon
SAVORY	4 teaspoons
GARLIC SALT	2-2/3 tablespoons
FLOUR	6 ounces
SOUR CREAM	1 gallon
MUSHROOMS, canned, sliced (with liquid)	1-1/4 quarts
ALMONDS, chopped, roasted	1 quart
SUGAR	1/3 cup
NOODLES, wide, cooked	6 quarts

Procedure

1. Sprinkle salt and pepper over veal. Brown meat and onions in butter.

2. Add water, savory and garlic salt; mix well. Cover and simmer 45 minutes or until meat is tender.

3. Blend flour and sour cream. Stir into veal mixture. Add undrained mushrooms, 1 cup of the almonds and sugar. Cook over low heat, stirring constantly, until thickened.

4. Serve over noodles. Garnish with almonds.

CELEBRITY CHOW MEIN

Popular with a melon ball appetizer and coconut custard pie.

Yield: 48 portions, ½ cup chow mein, ½ cup rice

Ingredients

CELERY	4 pounds
ONIONS, chopped	1 pound
BUTTER or MARGARINE	½ pound
BEEF, VEAL, CHICKEN or TURKEY, cooked	4 pounds
SOY SAUCE	½ cup
MUSHROOMS, sliced canned	8 ounces
WATER CHESTNUTS, sliced	8 ounces
MEAT STOCK*	2½ quarts
WORCESTERSHIRE SAUCE	2 teaspoons
FLOUR	1½ cups
MEAT STOCK*	1 quart
RICE, cooked	1½ gallons
CHINESE NOODLES, canned	1½ pounds

Procedure

1. Slice celery into diagonal slices about ¼ inch thick.
2. Saute celery and onions in butter until softened but not brown.
3. Cut meat or poultry into bite-size pieces.
4. Combine vegetables, meat, soy sauce, mushrooms, water chestnuts, first amount of stock and Worcestershire sauce. Cook until heated through, about 10 minutes. Check seasonings.
5. Blend flour with remaining stock. Add to hot mixture, cook and stir until slightly thickened.
6. Serve over hot rice. Top with Chinese noodles.

*Use stock same flavor as meat or poultry.

CREAMED HAM AND MUSHROOMS

Serve with a marinated whole green been salad and suggest sliced peaches with pistachio ice cream as the dessert.

Yield: 25 1-cup portions

Ingredients

CREAM OF MUSHROOM SOUP (canned)	3 quarts
TOMATO SAUCE	3 cups
GREEN PEPPERS, cut in slivers	1½ quarts
BUTTER or MARGARINE	6 ounces
HAM, cooked, diced	3 quarts
PATTY SHELLS	25
EGGS, hard-cooked, chopped	1½ cups

ALL AMERICAN FAVORITE CASSEROLE

A cup of hot consomme and a fresh fruit dessert combine with this entree for an inviting menu.

Yield: 24 1-cup portions

Ingredients

SPAGHETTI, ready-cut	1 pound
GROUND BEEF	3 pounds
CELERY, sliced	2 cups
ONION, chopped	1½ cups
TOMATO PASTE	1¾ cups
TOMATOES, canned, whole, undrained	2 quarts
SALT	5 teaspoons
OREGANO	1½ teaspoons
GARLIC POWDER	½ teaspoon
WHOLE KERNEL CORN (vacuum pack can) drained	3 cups
CHEESE, sharp processed American, cubed	½ pound
CHEESE, sharp processed American, shredded	¼ pound

Procedure

1. Cook spaghetti in boiling salted water until tender; drain.

2. Brown ground beef. Add celery and onion; saute until crisply tender but not brown. Pour off excess fat.

3. Add tomato paste, tomatoes and seasonings.

4. Combine hamburger mixture, spaghetti, corn and cubed cheese.

5. Portion into 24 individual casseroles or turn into 12-inch by 20-inch by 2-inch pan. Sprinkle with shredded cheese.

6. Cover. Bake in a 350°F. oven allowing 25 to 30 minutes for casseroles, 50 to 60 minutes for large pan.

▼   ▼

Procedure

1. Combine soup and tomato sauce; heat.

2. Saute peppers in butter 3 to 5 minutes.

3. Add peppers and ham to soup mixture. Let stand 10 to 15 minutes to blend flavors, keeping hot for service.

4. Serve in patty shells; garnish with chopped egg.

BEEF 'N OLIVE PIE

Present with a salad made of flat slices of iceberg lettuce spread with mayonnaise and topped with sliced cucumbers and a liberal sprinkling of parsley. An ice cream sundae can complete the meal.

Yield: 25 portions

Ingredients

BUTTER or MARGARINE	12 ounces
BEEF STEAK, round, cubed	10 pounds
DEHYDRATED CHOPPED ONION	½ cup
FLOUR	¾ cup
TOMATOES	1 No. 10 can
GREEN OLIVES, pimiento-stuffed, halved	3 cups
SALT	2 tablespoons
PEPPER	½ teaspoon
BISCUIT MIX	2½ pounds
MILK	2-2/3 cups
OLIVE HALVES (for garnish)	25

Procedure

1. Melt butter; add beef cubes and onion, brown.
2. Add flour; blend.
3. Gradually add tomatoes, cooking and stirring until thickened. Add olives, salt and pepper.
4. Cover; simmer 1½ hours or until beef is tender.
5. Fill individual casseroles.
6. Combine biscuit mix and milk, mixing lightly. Turn out on lightly-floured board; knead gently.
7. Roll out to ¼-inch thickness. Cut rounds to fit casseroles. Cut a 1¼-inch hole in center of each round. Place on top of filled casseroles.
8. Bake in a 450°F. oven 15 minutes, or until browned and crust is done. Garnish with ½ stuffed olive, placing in center hole.

Beef 'n Olive Pie

Spanish Green Olive Commission

PIMIENTO AND CHEESE TOPPED HASH PIE

The alternate triangles of red pimiento and yellow cheese create an eye-catching pinwheel effect. A "side" of celery hearts and pickles and a dish of maple walnut ice cream make this a meal "to write home about!"

Yield: 18 portions

Ingredients

ROAST BEEF HASH	1 No. 10 can
GREEN PEPPER, chopped	½ cup
ONION, chopped	½ cup
BUTTER or MARGARINE	3 tablespoons
PIMIENTO, chopped	½ cup
CHILI POWDER	¾ teaspoon
PASTRY TART SHELLS, 5-inch, baked	18
CHEESE, AMERICAN PROCESS	9 slices
PIMIENTOS, whole	12 to 14
COOKING OIL	as needed

Procedure

    1. Heat hash until warm throughout but not browned.

    2. Saute green pepper and onion in butter until tender.

    3. Add sauteed vegetables, chopped pimiento and chili powder to hash. Toss lightly to mix.

    4. Fill tart shells with warm hash mixture.

    5. Cut cheese and whole pimientos into wedge shaped pieces. Cover tops of pies with alternating pieces of pimiento and cheese. Brush lightly with oil.

    6. Bake in a 400°F. oven until cheese melts and hash is thoroughly hot.

GLAZED LUNCHEON LOAF ══════════

Companionable items include escalloped potatoes, raw spinach salad and red cherry pie.

Yield: 48 portions

Ingredients

CANNED LUNCHEON MEAT	6 pounds
SUGAR, brown (packed measure)	1-1/2 cups
FLOUR	1/3 cup
MUSTARD, dry	1-1/2 teaspoons
GINGER, ground	1/2 teaspoon
CLOVES, ground	1/2 teaspoon
VINEGAR	1/3 cup

SWEET AND SOUR PINEAPPLE PORK

Serve on a bed of fluffy hot rice and accompany with a salad of romaine, cress and avocado.

Yield: 80 portions

Ingredients

BONELESS PORK SHOULDER, cut in 1-inch cubes	20 pounds
COOKING OIL	½ cup
ONIONS, sliced	3¾ pounds
GREEN PEPPERS, 1-inch by ¼-inch strips	1½ pounds
CELERY, sliced	3 pounds
PINEAPPLE CHUNKS	1 No. 10 can
SUGAR, light brown	14 ounces
CORNSTARCH	8 ounces
VINEGAR, cider	1 quart
WATER	3 quarts
PINEAPPLE JUICE	1 No. 10 can
PINEAPPLE SYRUP (drained from chunks)	1 quart
SOY SAUCE	¾ cup

Procedure

1. Brown pork in oil. Cover; simmer until nearly tender, about 45 minutes. Pour off excess fat.
2. Add onions, green peppers and celery to pork; cook 5 minutes.
3. Drain pineapple chunks, reserving syrup.
4. Mix sugar and cornstarch. Combine with vinegar, water, pineapple juice, pineapple syrup and soy sauce. Stir into pork mixture.
5. Add pineapple chunks, cook, stirring carefully until sauce is smooth and thickened.

▼   ▼

Procedure

1. Slice luncheon meat into 48 slices, ¼-inch thick. Arrange in 3 rows (overlapping slices) in a 12-inch by 20-inch by 2½-inch pan.
2. Mix brown sugar, flour, mustard, ginger and cloves. Add vinegar; mix well.
3. Pour glaze over meat slices distributing evenly over rows.
4. Bake in a 375°F. oven 15 minutes or until heated through. Spoon glaze over meat slices before serving.

LAMB SALONIKA

*Feature with a green salad. And for dessert, offer a shortcake fashioned
with sponge cake, sliced peaches and almond whipped cream.*

Yield: 24 portions

Ingredients

FLOUR	1/2 cup
SALT	4 teaspoons
PEPPER	1/2 teaspoon
LAMB, leg or shoulder, trimmed, cut in strips or cubes	6 pounds
BUTTER	6 ounces
INSTANT GRANULATED GARLIC	1 teaspoon
ONIONS, chopped	2 cups
WATER	1-1/3 cups
CREAM OF CELERY SOUP, condensed	1 50-ounce can
MUSHROOMS, sliced	3 cups
SOUR CREAM	3 cups
CHIVES, chopped	3/4 cup

Procedure

1. Combine flour, salt and pepper; mix well. Dredge lamb in seasoned flour.

2. Melt butter; add lamb, garlic and onions. Cook over low heat until lamb is browned on all sides. Drain off excess fat, if necessary.

3. Add water, soup and mushrooms. Cook over low heat for 45 minutes, stirring occasionally.

4. Add small amounts of hot mixture to sour cream. Add warmed cream to the hot mixture being careful not to let it boil.

5. Add chives just before serving or sprinkle over top as garnish. Serve lamb on wild rice, white rice or noodles.

FRANKFURTERS AND SWEET KRAUT

Rye bread and baked apples a la mode make tasty partners for this "all-in-one" casserole.

Yield: 24 portions

Ingredients

BUTTER or MARGARINE, melted	8 ounces
ONIONS, chopped	2 cups
SUGAR, light brown (packed)	1-1/2 cups
CHILI SAUCE	2 cups
WORCESTERSHIRE SAUCE	1/3 cup
SAUERKRAUT, drained	1 No. 10 can
FRANKFURTERS, skinless	24
CHEESE, AMERICAN process, cut ½-inch by 4-inch strips	24 strips
BACON, partially cooked	12 slices
POTATOES, hot, mashed, seasoned	2 quarts

Procedure

1. Combine butter, onions, brown sugar, chili sauce and Worcestershire sauce; heat to boiling point.

2. Add sauerkraut; heat thoroughly.

3. Slit frankfurters lengthwise; place a strip of cheese inside pocket.

4. Place 2/3 cup hot kraut mixture in individual 8-ounce baking dishes.

5. Place a stuffed frankfurter on top.

6. Cut bacon slices in half. Place a piece of bacon across each frankfurter.

7. Pipe a border of potatoes around top of baking dish, close to edge.

8. Run under broiler until potatoes are brown and stuffed frankfurters are thoroughly hot.

VEAL CACCIATORA

Offer with rice or buttered noodles and a salad of crisp greens tossed with a hint of fennel.

Yield: 80 portions

Ingredients

GREEN PEPPERS, chopped	1½ quarts
ONION, finely chopped	2 quarts
GARLIC, instant granulated	1 tablespoon
COOKING OIL	1½ cups
MUSHROOMS, sliced, undrained	6 8-ounce cans
TOMATOES	1 No. 10 can
TOMATO PUREE	1¼ quarts
VINEGAR	½ cup
BAY LEAF, crumbled	1 small
SALT	¼ cup
PEPPER	2 tablespoons
FLOUR	2 pounds, 12 ounces
SALT	¼ cup
PEPPER	4 teaspoons
VEAL, boneless, 1/8-inch slices (3 ounces each)	30 pounds
PARMESAN CHEESE (optional)	as needed

Procedure

•1. Saute green peppers, onions and garlic in oil until tender.

2. Add mushrooms, tomatoes, tomato puree, vinegar, bay leaf and first amount of salt and pepper. Cover; simmer 30 minutes, stirring occasionally.

3. Combine flour and remaining salt and pepper. Dredge veal.

4. Grill meat on a well-greased grill until browned on both sides and meat is done. Place cutlets in steam table pans. Pour sauce over meat.

5. Sprinkle each portion with Parmesan cheese, if desired.

TAIPEH SPARERIBS

Rice teams easily with this dish. But you might try spoonbread or squares of not-too-sweet cornbread, by way of a change.

Yield: 24 portions, 3 quarts sauce

Ingredients

CLING PEACH SLICES	1 No. 10 can
PORK SPARERIBS	12 pounds
SALT	as needed
PEPPER	as needed
CELERY, coarsely diced	2 quarts
GREEN PEPPER, coarsely diced	1 quart
ONION, chopped	2 cups
COOKING OIL	½ cup
TOMATO SAUCE	2 quarts
VINEGAR	2 cups
SUGAR, light brown	12 ounces
PEACH SYRUP	2 cups
ROSEMARY LEAVES, crushed	2 teaspoons
BASIL, crushed	2 teaspoons
OREGANO, crushed	2 teaspoons

Procedure

1. Drain peach slices, reserving required amount of syrup.
2. Sprinkle spareribs with salt and pepper. Bake in a 350°F. oven 1½ hours.
3. Cook celery, green pepper and onion in oil until soft. Add tomato sauce, vinegar, sugar, syrup and herbs. Simmer 1 hour.
4. Drain fat from spareribs. Pour 1 quart sauce over ribs; top with drained peach slices.
5. Return to oven; heat 10 to 15 minutes. Keep remaining sauce hot; serve over ribs as desired.

LAMB AND FRUIT KEBAB CASSEROLE
A combination to delight the palate as well as the eye.

Yield: 50 portions

Ingredients

LEG OF LAMB, boneless	16 pounds
OIL AND VINEGAR DRESSING	2 quarts
SOY SAUCE	½ cup
JUICE FROM CANNED APRICOTS AND PINEAPPLE	2 cups
LEMON JUICE	¼ cup
BUTTER or MARGARINE	8 ounces
ALLSPICE	2 teaspoons
BANANAS	16 to 18
PINEAPPLE CHUNKS, drained	1 No. 10 can
APRICOT HALVES, canned, drained	50

Procedure

1. Cut lamb into 1½-inch cubes (16 to pound).

2. Combine dressing and soy sauce; pour over lamb; refrigerate 6 to 8 hours or overnight, turning occasionally.

3. Drain lamb. Heat marinade to simmering. Keep hot.

4. Combine fruit juice, lemon juice, butter and allspice. Heat to boiling. Keep hot.

5. Place marinated lamb cubes on shallow pans; broil until brown on one side; stir, continue broiling until done, basting occasionally with hot marinade.

6. Peel bananas; cut in 1-inch pieces. Arrange banana pieces, pineapple chunks and apricot halves in shallow pans. Brush with hot fruit juice mixture. Broil, brushing as needed, with more sauce, until glazed and beginning to brown lightly. Keep hot.

7. To serve, place about 5 cubes of lamb, 2 pieces of banana, a few pieces of pineapple and one apricot half in each individual casserole. Spoon a little of the hot marinade and some of the spiced fruit sauce over each casserole. Serve very hot.

Lamb and Fruit Kebob Casserole

American Lamb Council

PINEAPPLE VEAL IN TART SHELLS

Present with crisp-tender zucchini chunks and whole baby carrots.

Yield: 24 portions

Ingredients

VEAL STEAK, boneless, cubed	5 pounds
BUTTER	4 ounces
PINEAPPLE CHUNKS	1¼ quarts
SAUTERNE WINE	2½ cups
SALT	4 teaspoons
PEPPER	½ teaspoon
TARRAGON	2 teaspoons
GREEN ONIONS, chopped	12
CHICKEN BROTH	2 cups
MUSHROOMS, sliced (fresh)	1 quart
BUTTER or MARGARINE	4 ounces
CORNSTARCH	¼ cup
CHICKEN BROTH	2½ cups
PARSLEY, finely chopped	¼ cup
TART SHELLS, 3 to 4-inch, baked	24

Procedure

1. Saute veal quickly in butter to a rich brown.

2. Drain pineapple; add pineapple syrup and sauterne to veal. Add salt, pepper, tarragon, onion and first amount of broth. Cover; simmer meat until tender, about 45 minutes.

3. Saute mushrooms in remaining butter; add to meat.

4. Blend cornstarch and remaining broth; add to mixture; cook and stir until thickened.

5. Add pineapple chunks; heat slowly 5 minutes. Stir in chopped parsley.

6. Serve in baked tart shells.

SCALLOPED MEAT WITH EGGPLANT, TOMATO AND ONION

Garnish the plate with watermelon pickle arranged on chicory and complete the offering with jellied consomme madrilene and date nut bars a la mode.

Yield: 24 portions

Ingredients

EGGPLANT, medium	3 (4½ pounds)
SALT	4 teaspoons
ONION, chopped	4½ cups
TOMATOES, fresh, diced*	1½ quarts
BUTTER or MARGARINE	¼ pound
SALT	2½ tablespoons
PAPRIKA	1 tablespoon
PEPPER, ground black	¾ teaspoon
NUTMEG, ground	2 to 3 teaspoons
BEEF, lean, ground	3 pounds
PORK, lean, ground	1½ pounds
BREAD CRUMBS, soft	3 cups
BUTTER or MARGARINE, melted	3 ounces
CHEESE, sharp cheddar, grated	6 ounces (1½ cups)

Procedure

1. Wash eggplant; cut crosswise into ½-inch slices. Peel; sprinkle with first amount of salt. Set aside.

2. Saute onions and tomatoes in butter; add remaining salt, spices beef and pork. Mix well; cook until lightly browned.

3. Rinse salted eggplant in cold water; drain.

4. Place alternate layers of meat mixture and eggplant in a greased 12-inch by 20-inch by 2-inch baking pan, beginning and ending with meat mixture.

5. Cover pan closely with foil. Bake in a 350°F. oven 40 minutes.

6. Combine bread crumbs, melted butter and cheese; toss to mix.

7. Remove cover from pan; sprinkle with crumb mixture. Bake uncovered, 10 minutes or until brown.

*If fresh tomatoes suitable for cooking are not available, substitute 1¾ quarts canned chopped tomatoes, drained.

CHEESE PUFF BEAN BURGER PIE

Add a sliced orange and stuffed prune salad and double-deck sugar cookies filled with jelly.

Yield: 50 portions

Ingredients

GREEN BEANS, cut	1 No. 10 can
BEEF, ground, raw	8 pounds
SALT	2 tablespoons
PEPPER	½ teaspoon
SUGAR	2 tablespoons
MONOSODIUM GLUTAMATE	1 teaspoon
WORCESTERSHIRE SAUCE	2 tablespoons
HOT PEPPER SAUCE	½ teaspoon
ONION, chopped	1 cup
SHORTENING	6 ounces (¾ cup)
FLOUR	3 ounces (¾ cup)
TOMATOES, canned	3 quarts
MUSHROOMS, canned, sliced	1 pound
PREPARED BISCUIT MIX	1½ pounds
CHEESE, Cheddar, grated	¾ pound
MILK	2¼ cups
COOKING OIL	½ cup

Procedure

1. Drain beans.
2. Brown ground beef, adding fat only if there is not enough in the meat.
3. Add seasonings, onion, shortening and flour (the shortening may be omitted if sufficient fat cooks out from the meat to blend with the flour). Stir well.
4. Add tomatoes and mushrooms. Cook until slightly thickened. Add green beans.
5. Fill individual casseroles or disposable aluminum foil pie pans, allowing 6 ounces mixture for each.
6. Combine biscuit mix and cheese; add milk and oil. Mix to form drop biscuit dough.
7. Top hot meat mixture in casseroles with biscuit dough, using a scantily filled No. 30 scoop.
8. Bake in a 400°F. oven 20 minutes or until biscuit puffs are golden brown.

UPSIDE-DOWN HAM LOAF

Baked or mashed yams and French style green beans provide good support for this distinctive ham loaf.

Yield: 20 portions

Ingredients

FLOUR	1 tablespoon
SUGAR, brown (packed measure)	1 cup
CLOVES, ground	½ teaspoon
RAISINS, seedless	2 cups
CORNFLAKE CRUMBS	2 cups
EGGS, slightly beaten	4
GREEN PEPPER, chopped	¼ cup
ONION, chopped	¼ cup
HAM, ground	2 pounds
PORK, lean, ground	1 pound
VEAL, ground	1 pound
MILK	2 cups

Procedure

1. Combine flour, sugar and cloves; sprinkle evenly over bottoms of well-greased loaf pans.

2. Wash raisins; drain. Spread over sugar mixture.

3. Combine cornflake crumbs, eggs, green peppers, onions and ground meats in mixer bowl. Using paddle attachment, mix 1 minute at low speed. Do not overmix.

4. Add milk; mix 2 minutes more.

5. Place mixture in loaf pans, pressing lightly over raisins. Insert table knife at intervals into the meat to elininate any air pockets.

6. Bake in a 325°F. oven about 1½ hours. Remove from oven; invert on sheet pan leaving pan in place for a few minutes before lifting off.

7. Remove pans; allow loaves to firm 10 to 15 minutes before slicing.

MEAT LOAF BAKED IN SAUCE

Change-abouts with the sauce bring variety to this basic meat loaf. Try presenting with small white onions and peas, and with a frozen fruit salad as dessert.

Yield: 6 9-inch by 5-inch by 3-inch loaves or 2 12-inch by 20-inch by 2-inch pans.

Ingredients

BEEF, ground	8 pounds
PORK, ground	4 pounds
TOMATO SAUCE	1½ quarts
SALT	2 tablespoons
PEPPER	1 tablespoon
DRY MILK	1½ cups
EGGS, beaten	8
DRY BREAD CRUMBS or ROLLED OATS	1½ quarts
TOMATO SAUCE	1 No. 10 can
ALLSPICE	1 teaspoon
MACE	½ teaspoon
MINT FLAKES	1½ tablespoons

Procedure

1. Combine ground meats, first amount of tomato sauce, salt, pepper, dry milk, eggs and crumbs. Mix well.

2. Shape into six 9-inch by 5-inch by 3-inch pans.

3. Combine remaining tomato sauce with allspice, mace and mint flakes. Pour about 1¼ cups over each loaf. Reserve rest to heat and serve with loaves as extra sauce.

4. Bake in a 375°F. oven 1 hour.

SAUCE VARIATIONS

NO.1

TOMATO SAUCE	1 No. 10 can
SOY SAUCE	1/3 cup
PARSLEY FLAKES	2 tablespoons

NO.2

TOMATO SAUCE	1 No. 10 can
TARRAGON	1 tablespoon

INDEX

CHEESE DISHES
Cheese-Ham Souffle ... 19
Cheese Strata, Baked ... 25
Chipped Beef and Cheese Strata ... 18
Cottage Cheese Fondue ... 23
Cottage Cheese Pancakes ... 18
Pizza ... 20
Quiche Lorraine ... 24
Tomato-Onion Rarebit ... 22

EGG DISHES
Deviled Eggs in Pimiento Sauce ... 53
Egg Croquettes ... 43
Eggs Agemono ... 52
Eggs Florentine ... 48
Eggs Scandia ... 50
Eggs Supreme a la Creme
on Noodle Squares ... 42
French Toast with
Strawberry Butter ... 49
Frittata Lombardy ... 51
Goldenrod Eggs in
Pimiento Petal Shells ... 45
Mushroom Omelet ... 46
Noodle Squares, Baked ... 42
Tomato-Egg Scramble ... 44
Village Ham 'N Eggs ... 44

FISH AND SEAFOOD
Broccoli and Tuna Au Gratin ... 149
Cheesed Mashed Potatoes
with Broiled Fillet ... 156
Codfish Balls ... 168
Crab Biscayne ... 154
Crab Cakes ... 162
Crab Quiche, Alaska King ... 155
Fish Fillets with Puffy
Cheese Sauce, Baked ... 148
Fish on Tomato-Parmesan
Stuffing, Baked ... 153
Fish Patties, Baked ... 144
Fish Portions Mornay ... 154
Flounder, Rolled, with
Green Goddess Dressing ... 166
Halibut in Sour Cream, Baked ... 160
Salmon Crepes Bayou ... 167
Salmon Loaf, Baked ... 147
Salmon Mousseline ... 146
Salmon Pie, Savory ... 164
Scallop Casseroles, Individual ... 148
Scallops Marseilles ... 160
Seafood, Sherried ... 161
Seafood Special, Deviled ... 145
Shrimp and Pineapple,
Polynesian ... 158
Shrimp Creole ... 165
Shrimp Curry ... 169
Shrimp Dewey ... 163

Shrimp Rarebit, Gloucester ... 150
Tuna and Potatoes Au Gratin,
Scalloped ... 150
Tuna Chop Suey ... 151
Tuna, Eggs and Olives,
Escalloped ... 159
Tuna Stroganoff ... 152

MEAT
Beef Loaf, Vegetable ... 186
Beef 'N Olive Pie ... 196
Casserole, All American Favorite ... 195
Cheese Puff Bean Burger Pie ... 208
Chipped Beef and Eggs
en Casserole, Creamed ... 172
Chipped Beef, Deluxe Creamed ... 174
Chow Mein, Celebrity ... 194
Corned Beef and Cabbage Rolls ... 188
Corned Beef Hash with Peaches ... 184
Cornbread and Sausage ... 180
Frankfurter Meal-In-One ... 191
Frankfurter Ramekins,
Savory Olive ... 176
Frankfurters and Sweet Kraut ... 201
Green Beans and Veal,
Curried ... 187
Hamburger Stroganoff ... 179
Ham 'N Asparagus Casserole ... 173
Ham Loaf, Upside-Down ... 209
Ham and Mushrooms, Creamed ... 194
Ham Shortcake, Southern ... 180
Hash Pie, Pimiento and
Cheese Topped ... 198
Lamb and Fruit Kebab Casserole ... 204
Lamb with Grapes, Curried ... 185
Lamb Salonika ... 200
Lamb Shoulder Chops,
Garden Court ... 177
Luncheon Loaf, Glazed ... 198
Meat with Eggplant, Tomato
and Onion, Scalloped ... 207
Meatballs in Gingersnap Sauce ... 182
Meat Balls, Porcupine ... 192
Meat Loaf Baked in Sauce ... 210
Meat Loaf, Italian, Baked ... 190
Meat Loaf, Swedish, with
Onion Sauce ... 175
Pork Hash, Creamy ... 176
Pork, Sweet and Sour Pineapple ... 199
Shortribs, Apple Braised ... 172
Spareribs, Taipeh ... 203
Steak Strips with Soya Sauce ... 186
Sweetbreads with Chipped Beef
and Almonds, Creamed ... 183
Swiss Steak, Quincy House ... 178
Veal Cacciatora ... 202
Veal and Mushroom Casserole ... 193

Veal in Tart Shells, with
Pineapple   206
Weiners, Western   174
PASTA AND RICE
Beef Rice Casserole   63
Beefy Macaroni Casserole   57
Chicken and Noodles, Baked   60
Chicken Risotto   60
Chipped Beef and Noodle Casserole   75
Clam Pantry Pasta   70
Deviled Ham and Rice   57
Fiesta Rice 'N Cheese   78
Fish, Noodles and Mushrooms   71
Fish Tetrazzini   68
Lasagne, Easy   72
Lobster-Rice Casserole
with Sherry Sauce   76
Macaroni and Olives Au Gratin,
Baked   61
Manicotti, Stuffed, Hunter Style   58
Noodle and Applesauce Bake   64
Noodle Quiche with
Savory Salmon Sauce   56
Rice Croquettes with Hot
Spiced Applesauce   79
Rice Pancakes   59
Salmon-Noodle Bake   65
Shrimp Pilaf   69
Tomato Rice Au Gratin   62
Tuna and Noodles Au Gratin,
Baked   64
Tuna Casserole Supreme   62
Tuna Tetrazzini   66
Turkey and Ham Tetrazzini   74
POULTRY
Brunswick Stew   128
Chicken and Mushroom Duchesse,
Creamed   139
Chicken and Noodles, Scalloped   140
Chicken Divan   134
Chicken 'N Biscuit Pie   130
Chicken Supreme   136
Country Captain   135
Orange Barbecued Chicken Wings   141
Raisin Chicken California   138
Sesame Fried Chicken Breasts   137
Sherried Celery and Chicken
Oriental   132
Sweet and Sour Pineapple
Turkey   129
Turkey a la Queen   141
Turkey and Rice Barbecue   131
Turkey and Stuffing, Scalloped   136
Western Barbecue Chicken   130
SALADS
Beef Salad Bowl, Frizzled   120
Chef's Salad Bowl   125

Chicken or Turkey Salad   107
Chicken Salad Tarts Veronique   123
Cold Meat Festival Salad   114
Cottage Cheese Salad Loaf   121
Crab Louis   115
Crabmeat Rice Salad   116
Egg Salad, Jellied   116
Ham Pineapple Luncheon Salad   108
Kidney Bean and Frankfurter
Salad   107
Lamb Salad, Sportsman's   112
Orange-Shrimp Macaroni Salad   106
Rock Lobster Salad Supreme   117
Salad of the South Seas   112
Salmon or Tuna Mold   111
Seafood and Pineapple Salad,
Curried   118
Seaman's Salad   124
Shrimp, Rice and Lima Salad   125
Shrimp Salad, Chinese   119
Tartar Salad   122
Tomato Aspic Pie with
Vegetable Cheese Topping   110
Tuna and White Grape Salad
in Pastry Shells   120
Tuna Salad   106
Vegetable Potato Salad   109
SANDWICHES
Bacon-Avocado Club Sandwich   82
Cheese and Deviled Egg Sandwiches   84
Cheese and Frankfurter Sandwiches,
Open   87
Cheese Barbecue Sandwich   86
Cheese Buns, Western   103
Chicken Sandwich Au Gratin   92
Chili Burgers   84
Comin' Thru the Rye   85
Dutch Treat Plate   103
Fishwich—6 League   100
Ham and Egg Wiches   95
Ham-Cheese Sandwich   94
Ham 'N Cheese Sandwiches,
Grilled   94
Ham Sandwich, German Style   83
Ham Sandwich with Creamy
Cole Slaw Topping, Open   83
Hamburger Sandwiches, Barbecued   82
Mushroom Beef Burgers   102
Mushroom Sandwich,
French Toasted   93
Mustard Ham Sandwich Filling   96
Olive Cheese Burgers   98
Pineapple French Toast
Sandwiches   87
Pineapple Shrimp Luau Sandwich   101
Polynesian Hamburgers   90
Salmondilly Sandwich   88

Sauerkraut-Cheese Topped
Frankfurter Sandwiches 85
Steak Sandwich Diane 90
Swiss-Turkey Sandwich 86
Tuna and Cheese Sandwich,
Baked 98
Tuna Buns, Barbecued 99
Tuna-Cheese Club Sandwich 92
Turkey and Asparagus Sandwich
Au Gratin, Baked 91
SOUP
Cape Cod Fish Chowder 12
Chicken Vegetable Chowder 15
Continental Cream 6
Corn Chowder 10
Fish-Corn Chowder 8
Garnishes 7, 12
Ham Chowder 7
Irish Soup Dinner 4
Italiano Tomato Soup 14
Mulligatawny Soup 13
New Orleans Gumbo 11
Old-Fashioned Bean 10
Oriental Chicken Soup Dinner 6

Potato Chowder 14
Scallop Stew 5
Seafood Chowder 4
VEGETABLE ENTREES
Applesauce Sweet Potatoes 29
Beans and Franks, Tropical 29
Beans, Apples and Frankfurters,
Baked Casserole 34
Beans, Baked Idaho Style 31
Beans, Baked with Apricots 28
Corn and Cheddar Pudding, Fresh 39
Lima Beans, Creole 32
Lima-Ham-Pimiento Scallop 34
Mushroom Quiche, Fresh 38
Pizza Potato Pie 30
Potatoes with Cheese, Scalloped 35
Ripe Olive Onion Tarts 33
Tomato Cheese Fondue 35
Vegetable and Bacon Bake 36
Vegetable Souffle 37
Vegetable Stuffed Green Peppers,
with Tongue 28
Yam and Peanut Croquettes 32